Touch Rugby Tactics

Mastering the Game

Ken Handley

© Copyright 2023 - All rights reserved.

The content contained within this book may not be reproduced, duplicated or transmitted without direct written permission from the author or the publisher.

Under no circumstances will any blame or legal responsibility be held against the publisher, or author, for any damages, reparation, or monetary loss due to the information contained within this book, either directly or indirectly.

Legal Notice:

This book is copyright protected. It is only for personal use. You cannot amend, distribute, sell, use, quote or paraphrase any part, or the content within this book, without the consent of the author or publisher.

Disclaimer Notice:

Please note the information contained within this document is for educational and entertainment purposes only. All effort has been executed to present accurate, up to date, reliable, complete information. No warranties of any kind are declared or implied. Readers acknowledge that the author is not engaged in the rendering of legal, financial, medical or professional advice. The content within this book has been derived from various sources. Please consult a licensed professional before attempting any techniques outlined in this book.

By reading this document, the reader agrees that under no circumstances is the author responsible for any losses, direct or indirect, that are incurred as a result of the use of the information contained within this document, including, but not limited to, errors, omissions, or inaccuracies.

Table of Contents

INTRODUCTION 1

CHAPTER 1: TOUCH VS. TRADITIONAL RUGBY 5
- WHAT'S THE DIFFERENCE? 5
- FIELD SIZE 6
- RULES 6
- PLAYERS 9
- GAMEPLAY STRATEGY 10

CHAPTER 2: FUNDAMENTALS OF TOUCH RUGBY 13
- UNDERSTANDING THE BASIC RULES AND REGULATIONS OF THE GAME . 13
- KEY RULES TO KNOW AS A PLAYER 13
- KEY RULES TO KNOW AS A VIEWER 16
- POSITIONS AND ROLES 18
  - *What are the Various Player Positions and Responsibilities* 19
  - *Why Positions and Responsibility are Important in Gameplay* 22
- THE IMPORTANCE OF TEAMWORK 23
  - *What is Essential for a Successful Team?* 23
- COORDINATION AND TEAMWORK DRILLS 26
  - *Passing Lines* 26
  - *Interception* 26
  - *Evasion Skill Circuit* 27

CHAPTER 3: OFFENSIVE STRATEGIES 29
- HOW TO PLAY A SUCCESSFUL OFFENSIVE GAME 29
- HANDLING THE BALL—OFFENSIVE TECHNIQUES 30
  - *Passing Strategies* 32
  - *Offloading Strategies* 33
  - *Sub Box* 34
- SCORING ON THE OFFENSE 35
  - *Reading the Opposition and Finding the Gaps* 35

Scoring Plays.. 37
UNPREDICTABILITY ON THE FIELD—ADAPTING ON THE FLY 38

CHAPTER 4: DEFENSIVE STRATEGIES 41

BENEFITING FROM A STRONG DEFENSE 41
TECHNIQUES TO PREVENT SCORING 42
TAGGING TECHNIQUES AND PRACTICES 44
DECIPHERING THE OPPONENTS' GAMEPLAY................................... 46
KEYS TO A SOLID DEFENSIVE LINE 47

CHAPTER 5: SET PLAYS AND STRATEGIES 49

ADAPTING FROM OFFENSE TO DEFENSE TO OFFENSE 49
STRATEGIC TIMING 50
SWITCHING AND THE CUT PASS... 52
PLAYER WIDTH AND SPACING 53
PUMP FAKE 54

CHAPTER 6: CONDITIONING FOR TOUCH RUGBY 57

HOW TO TAKE YOUR GAME TO THE NEXT LEVEL IN TOUCH RUGBY 57
PHYSICAL REQUIREMENTS OF TOUCH RUGBY: A COMPREHENSIVE GUIDE
.... 59
EXERCISES TO FOSTER SPEED AND AGILITY.................................... 62
UNLOCKING OF STRENGTH AND POWER 66
The Development of Strength and Power Training Routines for Touch Rugby.. 67
THE ART OF WARMING UP 69
THE IMPORTANCE OF AN ADEQUATE COOL DOWN 72

CHAPTER 7: MENTAL ASPECTS OF THE GAME 75

GAME AWARENESS 75
READING YOUR TEAMMATES.. 77
READING THE OPPOSITION... 79
MENTAL TOUGHNESS 81
GOAL-SETTING AND VISUALIZATION: THE POWERFUL PAIR FOR SPORTS
EXCELLENCE 83
What Benefits Can Athletes Gain From Creating Goals?. 84

CHAPTER 8: ADVANCED TACTICS AND STRATEGIES 87

    Attacking Plays: Concepts and Ideas for the Offense.............. 87
    Defensive Plays: Neutralizing the Opposition 94

CHAPTER 9: GAME ANALYSIS AND IMPROVEMENT 99

CONCLUSION.. 105

REFERENCES.. 109

Introduction

Touch rugby is the most recent version of rugby and part of a great family of team sports we call "football." Actually, it's *the* great family of team sports. We can trace its origins in ancient Greece and two team ball games called *episkyros* and *faininda*, which later inspired the Roman *harpastum*, games surprisingly similar to modern rugby. Then, in medieval England, Scotland, and Italy, and always more countries in the modern era. Not only that, rugby football is the father of some of the most popular and financially robust modern sports worldwide, such as soccer (international football), basketball, and American football.

And then came touch rugby. Beginning as early as the mid-1950s, touch rugby, or simply Touch, was initially played by kids in playgrounds of Northern England inner schools. Because of the asphalt, it was not safe to play traditional rugby in those playgrounds, so teachers and students invented a version of the game with less contact and falling to the ground. However, for some years, this new version of rugby was not a real distinct sport.

That changed in 1968 when the South Sydney Touch Football Club was founded in Australia by Bob Dyke and Ray Vawdon and held the first official tournament. The new sport remained connected to traditional rugby since it was used as a training method for the Rugby League. Moreover, it gave former rugby players the opportunity to continue competing not only privately but also in an organized sport, as the rules of touch rugby made it more accessible to retired rugby players and younger players alike. That will become more clear in the next chapters.

In 1972, the founding fathers of touch rugby founded the New South Wales Touch Association and, finally, the Australian Touch Association six years later.

Touch rugby has surpassed its roots as simply "rugby for kids" or training tool. For rugby players, it was first a means of providing a more secure environment in which to hone their skills. However, it has since developed into a sport in its own right, winning the hearts of players of all ages and ability levels.

We can say that the origins of touch rugby may be traced back to a pragmatic training approach that enabled young rugby players and fans to improve their game without the inherent dangers that are connected with full-contact situations. It acted as a bridge between the development of skills and the rigorous requirements of traditional rugby, which was particularly popular among students.

Touch rugby is currently recognized and governed as a separate athletic discipline by international organizations and federations.

Touch rugby captures the core of the roughness that is characteristic of rugby while greatly reducing the hazards that are inherently linked with full-contact matches. Touch rugby has been welcomed by rugby clubs all around the globe, and members of these clubs have formed specialized teams that participate in leagues and tournaments.

One of the most appealing aspects of touch rugby is the natural protectiveness of the sport. Although it is not completely non-contact, as we'll see much better in the following chapters, the amount of intentional collisions is far lower than the hard tackles that are common in traditional rugby. The safety profile of touch rugby makes it an appealing choice for players who are looking for a lower-risk alternative. This is particularly true for players who have reached retirement age from full-contact rugby but still have a strong desire to remain connected to the sport, female players, younger players, or simply people who love the rugby sport but prefer its aspects of speed, agility, and ball movement, instead of the more hustle and muscle ones.

In other words, touch rugby is made for being inclusive, and it's one rare case of a sport with mixed-gender teams. These teams cultivate a feeling of camaraderie, and they are important also because they break down obstacles that may discourage new players from joining the sport.

Touch rugby extends beyond the confines of the playing field, providing a lively social component that adds an additional dimension of pleasure to the sport. It is important to highlight the sense of community that pervades this dynamic form of the game, which has led to an increase in the popularity of leagues and tournaments that are specifically devoted to touch rugby.

Whether you're an experienced coach, a veteran player, or a sportsperson just beginning your journey into touch rugby, you will benefit a lot by studying the game and deepening your theoretical knowledge. That includes fans, too, who often are on the verge of becoming more involved with the sport or are interested in understanding touch rugby at a deeper and more expert level. Regardless of the category you are in, the next chapters will make your touch rugby experience more complete and exciting.

Chapter 1:

Touch Vs. Traditional Rugby

You've got to get your first tackle in early, even if it's late.

–Ray Gravell

For the purpose of this book, we will use the term "Traditional Rugby" when talking about the codes of rugby union and rugby league. Both codes are equally exciting in their own format; however, this book is primarily about Touch Rugby.

What's the Difference?

First of all, we must put the record straight that the difference between touch and traditional rugby is not just contact. It's much more! Even though touch rugby's less harsh contacts are the first thing that comes to mind and the first thing anyone would see after watching a few minutes of play, there are, in fact, differences in every aspect of the game. In this chapter, we'll see all those points that differentiate the versions of the game of rugby.

Field Size

The size of the fields is considerably different between touch and traditional rugby. Touch rugby fields are typically smaller, ranging from 50 to 70 meters in length and 30 to 50 meters in width, while traditional rugby fields go from 100 to 120 meters in length and 68 to 70 meters in width.

Besides the size difference, there are more points where we can see the touch rugby field being different to the traditional one. Traditional rugby fields are, as we know, made of natural grass. Touch rugby fields, on the other hand, can be either from natural grass or artificial turf. Natural surfaces tend to be more dynamic and unpredictable, and artificial surfaces can give more speed and precision to gameplay. Touch rugby has the best of both worlds. That includes the general adaptability and accessibility of touch rugby, which can be played in various places, like parks, beaches, and indoor gyms, by people of all skill levels. One very noticeable difference between a Touch Rugby field and fields in other forms of rugby is that you will not see any goalposts on a Touch Rugby pitch, as there is no need to kick conversions or penalties.

Rules

Differences in rules tend again to make touch rugby more accessible to people of all skill levels, as it approaches physical contact differently. This is the point where the difference in contact comes into play.

Traditional rugby is known worldwide as the toughest ball sport when it comes to physical contact. There are tackling and hard touches all the time and a high risk of injury.

Nothing of all this is true for touch rugby. In touch rugby, tackling is not allowed, and contact is far less aggressive. For that reason, rules are fewer in number and simpler, as there is no need for complex rules that put tackling techniques in order, like in traditional rugby, since all tackling styles and techniques are forbidden altogether. This is another reason that touch rugby is more accessible and easy to play for more people, as it does not require a very fit physical condition and resistance to hard contact. That last condition is also favored by the simple fact that a touch rugby game's total duration is 40 minutes while a traditional rugby game is typically 80 minutes, with most of the players actually playing the whole 80 minutes, whereas, in Touch Rugby, the players are able to rotate in and out of play without any limitations on the number of rotations, but there are rules in place whereby the players have to interchange through the sub box legally. We will learn more about the sub-box in a later chapter.

Another difference in rules is that traditional rugby permits scrums, rucks, and mauls, while in touch rugby, they are not allowed. Indeed, scrums, rucks, and mauls make up a great part of the game in traditional rugby, as players engage in precise set formations to contest possession of the ball, often in very physical ways. However, this is not part of touch rugby, where the players always keep a certain distance between them, physicality is much less, the pace of the game is typically faster, and the style is more continuous, without frequent breaks.

This last aspect of touch rugby, the fast pace and rhythm of the game, is also encouraged by the time limit rule. Every team has at their disposal a precise number of touches, usually six, and then possession turns to the other team. This doesn't exist in traditional rugby (rugby union), where possession is determined exclusively by the ability of a team to maintain control of the ball with continuous passing, running, rucks, and mauls. So, in touch rugby, the focus of a team is to conclude its actions as soon as possible, or in any case before the limit takes possession of the ball away, while in traditional rugby, a team can build its entire style of playing on ball possession.

Touch is the magic word of the entire story. Touch rugby is called this way because touching the opponent lightly is the only contact allowed in the game. By touching the ball carrier, the defending team stops the attacking team's play. The ball carrier may also choose to touch a defender, causing the referee to acknowledge the touch, while shouting out the relevant touch number 1 through 6 and stop the action. Then, the attacking team has to begin their attack again with a roll ball. As we said, if the defending team manages to touch the opponent's ball carrier six times, that is, interrupt their attack six different times, the attack of the other team ends for good. Possession passes to the defending team, which now becomes the attacking team.

We said "roll ball." This is another difference in rules, as roll ball is how action begins again after a touch from the defending team or ball carrier in touch rugby. The ball carrier puts the ball down between his or her legs and rolls it with his or her hand to another player of the team who is behind the current ball carrier. The second player takes possession of the ball and either runs with the ball, avoiding contact or passes it immediately so the attack can continue. On the contrary, in traditional rugby, players engage in physical rucks to contest the possession.

Last but not least, another important difference has to do with scoring. In traditional rugby, a team scores by successfully grounding the ball in the opponent's in-goal area or by kicking it through the goalposts. On the contrary, in touch rugby, a team scores only by grounding the ball in the opponent's area, and just as in traditional rugby, the try line also counts as the ingoal area.

Players

In touch rugby, the standard number of players is 14 per team, with only six players on the field at a given time. In traditional rugby, each team typically has 13/15 players on the pitch, depending on which code is being played. This difference comes along with those previously mentioned, as touch rugby is played on smaller fields, has a faster pace, and has a more open playing style with far less physical contact. On the other hand, traditional rugby, with more players on the field, has a great concentration of players that contest the ball possession in more dynamic and intense ways.

Touch rugby is related more to quick bursts of energy and requires agility and, hopefully, fitness from players, as touch rugby is faster-paced and less physical. At the same time, traditional rugby requires more enduring physical effort for a long duration, strength, and endurance to harsh contacts.

Besides the changes in the style of play, the difference in the players' numbers also creates differences in the players' positions and the tactics followed by the teams. As we'll see also in the following section, in touch rugby, all players must attack and defend, while in traditional rugby, there are more precise positions.

Gameplay strategy

Touch and traditional rugby have common roots; however, the different rules and characteristics we briefly saw also give different gameplay strategies. Gameplay strategy in touch rugby revolves around speed and agility, while in traditional rugby, the most essential elements are physicality and team cohesion.

More precisely, the smaller team and field size makes versatility very important for touch rugby players, who must be able to both attack and defend. On the other side, in traditional rugby, players are assigned more specialized positions, such as forwards and backs, and each of them has a unique role on the field.

In touch rugby, emphasis is given to quick and accurate ball movement in order to maintain momentum. The teams are trying to circulate the ball by passing it fast to create openings in the defense by disorientating the opponents. In traditional rugby, a team uses set-piece plays, such as scrums and lineouts, as restarts after stoppages to contest possession and gain territory, setting up its tactics. A fundamental element of the game in traditional rugby is kicking, as teams use kicks to gain territory and force the opponent team into the defensive position. There are box kicks, chip kicks, and grubber kicks, used as options in open play. There are also penalty kick to the sideline, penalty shot at goal and dropouts from the 22 m line and the goal line. These kicks in traditional rugby can sometimes slow the pace of the game down and take away some of the game's excitement.

The defensive plays are also different according to the general aspects of each style of play. In traditional rugby, tackling is very important, and defense is based on creating compact bulks and line speeds, as rucking contributes to defending effectively. In touch rugby, the defensive structure is again important, but there are no compact bulks and tackling. The teams, when they defend, try to prevent gaps, exploit turnovers, and touch the ball carrier to halt the offense's progress.

In sum, for touch rugby, the most important elements are speed, agility, and simplicity, and it prioritizes adaptability and quick decision-making. In contrast, traditional rugby includes more complex and massive tactics, with set-piece plays, specialized positions, and physicality.

Chapter 2:

Fundamentals of Touch Rugby

Give blood! Play Rugby! -Unknown

Understanding the Basic Rules and Regulations of the Game

We've already briefly seen some rules and regulations of touch rugby in the previous chapter, compared with those of traditional rugby. In this chapter, we'll delve more into this version of rugby rules, both from the players' and the viewers' points of view.

Key Rules to Know as a Player

The five basic rules every player should know starting off in touch rugby are:

1. **Team size and substitutions:** Each team typically has six players on the field, and at least in some leagues, they can or must be mixed male and female. Age restrictions can

also categorize them. There are typically eight other players in the sub-box (on the bench). Substitutions can be made anytime from one side of the field, typically freely, without the referee having to give permission. Substituting players have just to make legal contact within the sub-box for the substitution to be completed with a penalty.

2. **Scoring:** A team scores a try when they manage to ground the ball behind or on the opponent's area, the try-line. In this way, they earn a point.

3. **Touches and roll ball:** A touch is the only contact allowed, and it's minimal contact between a defending player and the player who possesses the ball. For a play to be considered a touch, the referee must call it. After the touch, the attacking player must put the ball on the ground and restart their team's action with a roll ball, i.e., passing the ball to a teammate by rolling the ball with their hand to a teammate who is no more than 1 m behind them. There is also the possibility for the ball carrier to touch the defender with their hands or fingers. That may sound paradoxical, but a touch by the ball carrier can be a smart tactical move if they feel they can exploit a weakness in the defense. With the touch, they put the

ball on the ground and begin all over again with a roll ball.

4. **Turnovers and possession changes:** After six touches, possession changes, and the new attacking team begins playing with a roll ball of their own. A change in possession also occurs when the ball is dropped by a player or after a touch pass and when a player crosses the sideline without being touched.

5. **Penalties:** That happens in cases of forward passes, interferences with the rolling ball, offside play, obstruction, tackling, disrespectful treatment to another player or the referee, and, of course, a hard touch or a hit. When the referee awards a penalty, they then set the onside line for the defense. That means that the defending team has to go back 10 meters, with the attacking team earning territory and coming closer to the try line to get the point.

6. **Offside rules:** In touch rugby, a player is offside if they simply receive a forward pass. That means that every attacking move must begin with the player receiving the ball while they are behind it and not closer to the try line than the ball carrier. After a touch, the referee instructs the defensive players to retreat back

towards their own goal line seven meters from the point of touch If not all of them do so before the tap, those who haven't are offside. Also, the attacking players must be careful after a touch, as they must not be ahead of the tap marker, or else they are offside. The offside rules are important for the game's structure. They should learn to be careful not to pass the ball forward and to move, trying to find gaps and open spaces remaining behind the point of the ball carrier at any moment. They also must be ready to retreat quickly when touches happen.

Finally, another important element of the game is fair play. Players must avoid hard contact, verbal abuse, obstruction, and foul play. If their attitude does not respect fair play, they can be ejected from the game.

Key Rules to Know as a Viewer

The key rules a first-time viewer should know to avoid confusion are the ones already mentioned, plus a few more, such as the game is made of two halves of 20 minutes each with one minute of halftime, that when a female player scores, her team is awarded two points instead of one, and the way the standings are made in a championship, based on the points the teams win after the results of their matches.

The common point system is this: when a team wins, it gets three points, and the losing team gets one point; when there is a draw, each team wins two points; if a team forfeits a match, they get zero points. The points are allocated after each match and determine each team's position in the standings. It's noteworthy that in touch rugby, the losing teams get one point, and only the teams that forfeit matches get zero points. That shows us that touch rugby values and encourages competitiveness and competition regardless of the game's result. The only thing that isn't worth anything is not trying to field a team and dropping a game.

There are some previously mentioned rules we could specify for the first-time viewer. First is the touch, which is also called "tag." A touch occurs when an onside player of the defending team makes contact with the ball carrier or the ball carrier touches a defender whether that defender is onside or not. For the touch to be awarded, the referee must decide it, as the referee is responsible for officiating the match and making all final decisions. Nevertheless, the defending player can claim they made a touch by shouting "Touch" and raising their hand. In that case, the referee will have to decide if the touch truly occurred and whether or not to award it. When the referee awards the touch, the attacking player must restart the game with the roll ball at the point where the players touched each other. The ball carrier makes the roll ball, and the game restarts—that's the second rule we're explaining more. The player to whom the ball is headed then picks up the ball and either passes it to a teammate or runs with the ball avoiding contact and hopefully offloads the ball to a teammate who can then possibly score the try. The receiving player from a roll ball is called the dummy half. The dummy half can pass the ball further, run, or move with it as the game restarts. However, if the dummy half is tagged or touched by an onside player, then they lose possession of the ball to the opposition.

The third rule regards carrying the ball and scoring. We should specify that the ball carrier can go on, even if the defending player was off-side when the attacking team started their action. Off-side play is when, after a legal touch, the defending player does not retreat seven meters from the point of the touch.

Of course, we could go on. But it is better to say more, covering the various aspects of the game. We add right away that the touch rugby ball is unique. Touch rugby balls are designed to have maximum grip and be as easy to pass as possible, as kicking in official Touch Rugby is not allowed (the tap excluded). They are also just a bit above a size 4 in dimensions, making them far easier to handle for adults in particular than a standard rugby ball. These should not be used in standard rugby competitions unless size 4s are allowed.

Positions and Roles

Let's talk more precisely about the player's positions and roles.

What are the Various Player Positions and Responsibilities

In touch rugby, the player positions are more fluid and not fixed like in traditional rugby or sports like football (soccer) and basketball. In traditional rugby, there are props, hookers, fly-halves, and other positions. In contrast, in touch rugby, players do not have designated positions, and instead, they adapt their positions following the flow of the game. As we've seen, there aren't set pieces like scrums and lineouts, and that contributes to the fluidity of the positions, too.

Nevertheless, players can naturally take on different roles depending on their skills and style of play. They can be better ball carriers, focus on support play, create opportunities, or be better at the defensive end. Others can be better at handling the ball, faster, and more versatile on the offense, and others are more robust and capable of stopping the opponent's attacking actions and stealing the ball. The teams, based on the individual players' abilities and preferences, can create tactics and schemes. The players' positions in touch rugby are (two players in each role):

1. **Middles/Centers**: The middles are positioned in the middle of the field, and they act as playmakers, distributing the ball and trying to create opportunities for the offense to score.

2. **Wings**: The wings are positioned on the extreme edges of the field, close to the

sidelines. Their focus is to attack by exploiting open space on the edges of the playing area.

3. **Links**: The links are positioned between the centers and the wings. They primarily connect middles and wings, providing continuity for the attack and creating width.

The middles support both links and wings, giving passes that can result in attacking moves and directing the rhythm of the team's offense. When the team is defending, they organize the central part of the defensive line and make key touches to prevent the opponent from creating opportunities and flow in the attacking move. The wings use speed and agility to skip opponents to approach the try line and hopefully score by grounding the ball in there. The wings should also shout loudly the touch count as play progresses. In defense, their focus is to prevent similar moves toward their own try line by the attacking wings of the other team. The links are closer to the middles, and they are usually the first to receive the ball from them, offering passing options. They can pass the ball quickly in transition to the wings, giving them the opportunity to find a gap and attack. Defensively, the links cover the outer areas, and their role is crucial in keeping the line compact and preventing attackers' advancements.

Furthermore, we can break down possible roles in the following:

1. **Ball carrier**: The ball carrier is the player who initiates the attacking action of their team.

They carry the ball and make decisions about when to pass and how to conduct the team's maneuvers.

2. **Support runner**: The support runners position themselves to receive a pass from the ball carrier or the dummy half, thus offering options for the team's attacking action and hopefully finding a gap in the defensive line.

3. **Defender**: These are the players who specialize in preventing the opponents from scoring by stealing the ball and making touches on the ball carrier. They are good at maintaining and guiding the team's defensive line and closing gaps, too.

4. **Dummy runner**: The dummy runners are players who fake that they are about to receive the ball while they don't, acting as decoys and confusing the defenders. This way they open space for other players of their team to actually get the ball and attack the opponents' area.

5. **Strike runner**: These players come from behind to actually get the ball while running toward a gap in the defensive line to penetrate to the try area and get the point. They must be ready to receive the ball at the right time and place,

exploiting the dummy runners' decoy and the open spaces in the defensive line.

Why Positions and Responsibility are Important in Gameplay

Positions and responsibilities are crucial in all team sports for effective gameplay, and touch rugby could not be an exception. We can note a couple of precise points on their importance:

1. **Specialization**: We saw that while there are no fixed positions like in other sports, in touch rugby, there is nevertheless a specialization of roles as players have different skills and attributes. There are players who excel in one part of the game, let's say carrying and passing the ball, while others are better in other parts of the game, such as defending. A team should take notice and allow them to maximize their potential with specialized training and responsibilities.

2. **Strategic planning and gameplay**: Based on the abilities and roles of the players and the specialization process, a team should build their plans and gameplay in order to exploit them as much as possible, achieving the best performance level they can get to.

The Importance of Teamwork

Apart from allowing and helping players develop their unique skills and strengths, therefore giving them precise positions and roles, it's essential to make them work as a team. We have seen many times in sports history that teams made of individual great players fail in their goals because they didn't become a real team. Being a team is not just a sum of individual skills but creating additional qualities that exceed those of individual skills. On the contrary, lack of teamwork reduces the sum of individual skills of the players. If a team has great players but they don't play as a team, they will probably have worse results than a team with less capable players who make excellent teamwork.

What is Essential for a Successful Team?

1. **Team coordination**: Working on their skills and being given positions and roles is not enough for players. They also need to cooperate well and play in a coordinated way if they are to have the best possible results. To do so, they must understand their roles as part of a team effort and work in practice and inside the games to improve their communication, coordination and automatism, becoming like a legion or a machine that functions perfectly.

2. **Adaptability**: Having precise roles and playing in a coordinated way can enable players to adapt their game and tactics to changing situations during the match. We must always remember a team does not play by itself. There are the opponents, too. So, plans and roles must be able to adapt according to the situations and how the game is going. Players must be ready to do so, and knowing how to work as a coordinated team is crucial in facing difficult situations and bad momentum during the game.

3. **Offensive tactics**: Obviously, if you want to win, you have to score. So, there is no playing well without having effective offensive tactics that can bring you to score. That can be achieved through communication, well-timed passes, well-positioned running lines, coordinated plays with dummy runners and strike runners we've already seen, and many other things. The important point is to remember that, in the long run, individual talent is not enough to open and penetrate a defensive line in touch rugby.

4. **Defensive tactics**: If the team can sometimes get it done on the offense, thanks to great individual plays, even if teamwork is not perfect, that's impossible in defense. Great

defenders are very important, but they can't hold the entire line and be everywhere. While an attacker can penetrate the defense and carry the ball to the try area, a defender cannot cover all the possible gaps alone. That makes teamwork and tactical positioning essential to cover the field and prevent the attacking team from scoring. Players must be very attentive in guarding the opponent they have in front of them, but also the whole defensive line, and be coordinated with their teammates. Communication and defense are paramount.

5. **Effective substitutions**: Substitutions are crucial for two reasons. First, they can correct the team's game by putting on the field a player whose characteristics best fit the situation or the opponents. Secondly, they can bring more energy to the team by changing tired players or players on a bad day with fresh players who are hopefully in better shape on that day. The coaches must know their players very well and also study the opponents in order to make appropriate plans and effective substitutions.

Coordination and Teamwork Drills

We said that working on coordination is essential for a team in order to have better teamwork and eventually get the best possible results. It's time to see a few teamwork drills that can help coaches prepare their teams in that direction.

Passing Lines

Passing accuracy is crucial to the offense as it's necessary for maintaining possession, creating scoring opportunities, and avoiding turnovers that can easily give the ball to the opponents. Timing and communication are the bases for circulating the ball well. Here is a basic drill that can help with passing: Players form two lines, one as opposed to the other, passing a ball back and forth between them. They can introduce variations, like quick, long, and pop passes. It can also be important to establish some verbal cues in order to have more effective and rapid communication during the game.

Interception

The first goal of the defense is to steal the ball from the attacking team since that not only protects the team's area and prevents the opponents from scoring but also can create opportunities to counterattack and score for themselves. So, the point is to improve anticipation and interception abilities to improve the team's defensive effectiveness. A basic useful drill can be the following: Some players try to pass the ball to others across the field, and defensive players attempt to intercept it. The defending players must focus on positioning themselves, reading the movements of the offense, and working on the timing. The drill can become increasingly more difficult by introducing more attacking players and making the passes unpredictable. Note that this drill and the previous one can work both ways. It is simultaneously a drill for defense and interception but also to improve passing by the offense. The same is true for the previous one. The team works defense and offense at the same time, and the coach can also rotate players in both phases of the game.

Evasion Skill Circuit

Evasion Skill Circuit is a set of drills designed to make a player more able to overcome defensive play. Evading is crucial in touch rugby, as the ultimate aim of a player is to avoid being touched by a defender and maintain possession, looking for a pass or a run to the try area. An Evasion Skill Circuit can include drills with cone dribbling, mirror drill, sidestepping practice, reaction ball drills, and more. In cone dribbling, the players follow a zigzag pattern around a series of cones, dribbling the ball in and out of the cones, changing their direction. In a mirror drill, a player mimics the movements of the ball carrier, so they have to come up with unpredictable moves. In sidestepping practice, players work on fast direction changes, learning to keep balance while pushing the defenders off-balance with explosive direction changes. In reaction ball drills, players work with a ball player that moves unpredictably, getting used to adjusting fast in dynamic game situations.

Chapter 3:

Offensive Strategies

I think you enjoy the game more if you don't know the rules. Anyway, you're on the same wavelength as the referees.

–Jonathan Davies

How to Play a Successful Offensive Game

A successful offensive game in touch rugby requires various key tactics and abilities. We have already seen several of those in the previous chapters, but here, we will focus exclusively on the offense.

As a general rule, we can say that to be successful offensively, a team must have great communication, a good and quick passing game, and strong support play, with the ability to create gaps in the defense. Moving the ball with speed and accuracy allows catching defending players off guard to create open spaces for the attacking players. Doing that depends not only on the player who passes the ball but also on the one who receives the pass. Players must position themselves in the right way to get the ball and give options to the ball carrier. The whole team needs to be in a flow and move continuously, not just wait for the playmaker to create plays.

Variation of plays and tactics is also important, as successful offenses vary their style, and this way, they have more possibilities to find the winning play and confuse the defense. Different passes and types of ball movements, dummy runners, unpredictable choices, and schemes of attack can make all the difference.

For all that, communication between teammates is also crucial during the game, and it must be prepared well and coordinated during practice. The players must signal their intentions and call for the ball, which contributes to another important aspect, that is, awareness of the game. The attacking players must be aware of the situation, the touch count, the positioning of their opponents, and where they are on the field.

In the following paragraphs, we will see more about passing, offloading, finding gaps, reading the opposition, becoming unpredictable, and more useful tips on how to create scoring plays.

Handling the Ball—Offensive Techniques

In handling the ball, the most crucial plays a player should be technically equipped to do well are running lines, passing, offloading, evading with the ball, and executing the roll ball.

Running lines means running while holding the ball in two hands, as this usually doesn't give an indication of intent. There is no need to explain how fundamental this skill is as if you want to score, you must be able to run fast and reach the try line through gaps on the defense, and you obviously must carry the ball with you. Running lines can be crucial to open a gap for another player to break in after receiving a pass, for example, by running laterally to make defenders follow you and create open spaces. A player must work on having good control of the ball and the ability to make changes of direction without losing possession.

We said a lot about passing already, and we'll say much more later, so the importance of passing the ball well cannot be overestimated. The point is that you have to handle the ball very well in order to pass it efficiently. So, working on handling the ball to pass it right in every possible situation is mandatory for touch rugby players.

Offloading means passing the ball to a teammate just before being touched to avoid the touch. This is important to maintain continuity in the offensive action, especially if there is a good opportunity for the team to score. Offloading requires spatial awareness and timing, so players should work on quick plays in various scenarios to be ready. Working on communication is important in this case, too, to make sure that the player who receives the ball is also ready and has a good grasp on the ball, although receiving it is unpredictable.

Evasion skills are essential, and working on handling the ball during maneuvering to avoid being touched by defenders is necessary. We've already talked about the evasion skill circuit in the previous chapter. To add to that, for this play, it's crucial to do some footwork exercises, improve reaction time and cultivate the ability to create space. Having good movement down is crucial to maintain stability and the grasp on the ball. Unstable maneuvering can result in losing possession of the ball too.

Every attack begins with a roll ball, as we have previously explained. That creates two moves the players must work on. The first is putting the ball on the ground after getting touched. The second is picking it up and passing it immediately as a dummy half so the attack can proceed. Speed and precision are crucial in those moves in order for the attack to restart, giving a good tempo to the team's movement, hopefully before the defense is prepared and has closed the spaces. The team must work on the automatism of the roll ball, making the two moves many times during practice. It all comes down to communication and handling the ball well.

Passing Strategies

There can be different passing techniques, such as short, long, looping, and huge missed passes. When a team presents a variety in their passing game, they create more situations that could produce an opportunity to score. It also becomes more difficult for the defense to read their movements and intercept the ball or the play. Rapid and precise passes maintain the rhythm of the offensive action and, again, create opportunities to catch the defenders out of position.

A common tactic in touch rugby is, for example, passing the ball with long and wide passes, called huge missed passes. In this way, the attacking team tries to cut out multiple defenders while, at the same time, sometimes the pass skips other attacking players who are between the two players who play and receive the ball. With a huge missed pass, they can rapidly shift the point of attack, stretching the defense horizontally in order to catch it off guard and create the opportunity to penetrate and score.

The problem is defenses can anticipate such passes and steal the ball if they read the action correctly. Moreover, in order for the pass to create a scoring opportunity, other players of the attacking team must be ready to exploit the widened space created by the pass. This is an example of great communication and a strong tactic on which a touch rugby team should work in practice.

Offloading Strategies

Offloading is about maintaining possession and going on with the attack. In touch rugby, that means passing the ball just before being touched. Some examples of offloading strategies could be quick pass before contact, offload in traffic, flick pass, and switch pass. The goal is always to create a gap or open space in the opponent's defense, which the player who receives the ball can progress even closer to the try line and potentially score.

A quick pass in touch, that is, just before a touch, the ball is quickly passed to another teammate in better space, can create a lack of coordination and destabilize defense, as one defender is off position without managing to make the touch. Offload in traffic is deepening this strategy as the ball carrier, by faking to run towards the try line or to the wings, manages to draw the defensive line to him, not just one player but more, or its positioning in general, and in this way makes it lose its cohesion and stability, potentially creating opportunities for the other attacking players after passing them the ball.

A flick pass is when the ball carrier releases the ball to a nearby teammate with a wrist flick right before being touched. This is a precise technique players should work on in practice, as it can save the attacking maneuver of the team, although the ball carrier's body and hands are not in a position for a normal pass, which involves a complete arm movement. Finally, the switch pass is when the ball carrier offloads the ball to a teammate who is running an opposite running line. This move can be very effective because it's unpredictable, and the defense will often be caught off guard. On the other hand, it is perhaps the most difficult to perform, and it certainly will take a lot of practice for an individual player to be able to perform it in a real match, but also for the team to be in the position to utilize it.

Sub Box

In touch rugby, the sub box is the designated area where players can enter and exit from the field during the match. This is where the substitutions are made.

The role of the sub-box is to ensure that substitutions will be made in an organized and controlled manner without disrupting the flow of the game. The players must make clear calls or signals and communicate with the coaching staff and teammates. In that way, the changes are quick and accurate.

Obvious and easy as it may seem, using the sub-box correctly takes work, and drills in practice are essential. Things can become confusing, especially in cases of great pressure, where the substitutions have to be fast and efficient to keep up the team's tempo and not waste any precious time. Simulating similar scenarios during training will make players more comfortable with the process and will easily eliminate the possibility of messing up when every little detail can count.

Scoring on the Offense

We have already talked about communication, maneuvering fast and evading the defenders, passing the ball well to create opportunities, and supporting the attack with dummy runners and dummy strikers. Now, we'll focus on more precise ways to find gaps in the defense and exploit them.

Reading the Opposition and Finding the Gaps

Reading the opponent has to do not only with the field but also before the game, with studying and analyzing their game as much as possible, hopefully also through video analysis and using modern advanced performance analysis software and methods.

The first thing a coaching staff and a team should do is observe the opponent players' movement and positioning. If their defensive function is not a brilliant perfection, they will have weaknesses and spaces that are not so well covered. The attacking team should notice defenders who are out of position and attack those positions directly after quick and accurate passes.

Another possibility is for the opponent team to have excellent defensive positioning but not-so-quick players. In this case, the attacking team can point those not-so-quick players and attack them with fast, direct changes or with lateral movements.

Creating opportunities is not only a matter of the opponent's weaknesses but also of creative plays. The attacking team can create gaps even if initially they didn't exist, using deception tricks like the ones we've already seen (dummy runs) or schemes that can create numerical superiority in a particular area of the field. Naturally, the coaching staff and the players must work on those tricks and schemes during the training.

The evasion skills can be decisive in a situation such as the following example. Players often tend to run sideways and shift across the defense to find gaps, while on the other side, the defending players keep moving in order to reduce the possibility of penetration. That's why a good tactic would be for the attacking player to run straight so the defender has to commit to a post waiting for them. In that case, a quick direction change can fool the defender and allow the attacking player to let them behind, moving towards the try area.

Scoring Plays

Some more scoring plays are tap and accelerate, off-the-ball movement, and exploiting fatigue.

Tapping the ball quickly, while the defenders are not yet set onside, and accelerating toward the opponents can surprise the defense and give needed space and time to score.

Off-the-ball movement, that is, players moving and positioning themselves to give options to the ball carrier and receive passes, can disrupt the defensive line and create opportunities to score.

A factor always present in sports is fatigue. Even the most prepared and well-structured players will eventually suffer fatigue to some degree. A team must be ready first to recognize and then to exploit any signs of fatigue from the defense. A way to raise possibilities for that is by ball retention and a good passing game, which can provoke lapses among tired defending players.

The most basic offensive move in touch rugby, according to experts, is the "switch." In this tactic, there is the ball carrier who's running diagonally across the field while one of their teammates is running on the opposite diagonal. As they meet, the ball carrier passes the ball to the other player, opening a gap in their opponents' defensive line. A slightly more complex variant of the switch is the player who receives the ball, turns around, and begins to run the diagonal of the original ball carrier, while the latter provides outside support. Coaches and players have developed many other schemes related to the switch because it's a powerful move that, if applied successfully, creates the opportunity to score even if the defense knows how it works.

Another move is the "wrap," where the ball carrier gives the ball to another player, and then they run around behind the new ball carrier, trying to gain an overlap. Finally, diving toward the try line has become a common move in modern touch rugby, as the game's speed reduces the time the attackers have at their disposal to complete the attack and score before being touched by the defense.

Unpredictability on the Field— Adapting on the Fly

Dynamic communication among teammates on the field can be crucial, allowing them to identify gaps, exchange information, and make fast collective decisions during the game. To be able to do that, a team must work on establishing clear and concise signals and cues.

To become unpredictable and efficient, a team must work on quick decision-making drills in practice. The coaches can include simulations of scenarios where rapid decisions are necessary and keep working on them during training. In this way, when a similar moment arrives for real during a game, the players will be much more ready to act effectively and unpredictably.

The more a team works on developing versatile skills in players, the easier it will be for them to act unpredictably on the field and adapt on the fly during the game. Being able to fulfill various roles allows players to switch positions and provides more options to the coaching staff for developing surprising tactics the opponents will never see coming.

Another important training outside the field to be prepared for the difficulties of the field is psychological resilience. Mental toughness and resilience come with practice and automatism, learning to keep coming after the game and the opponent regardless of the momentum and the situation. A team that has developed the skill of not panicking and dissolving in difficult conditions can adapt to changes in the game and overcome bad moments.

Chapter 4:

Defensive Strategies

Don't hate the game, hate the player. – Unknown

Benefiting from a Strong Defense

A strong defense is the solid base upon which the success of a team can be built. That should be common sense since no matter how much you score, the opponent can score more if your defense is weak. However, if you minimize the opponent's scoring, the possibility of losing is reduced.

Fundamentally, a defense must continuously keep three things in mind: pressure, disruption, and stealing. By applying pressure and being defensively aggressive, a team causes problems for their opponent team's offensive play, not letting it unfold as planned or canceling it out altogether. Disruption means putting obstacles in the way and stopping the opponent's offensive schemes from concluding. The difference with pressing is that pressing goes after the offense aggressively, while disruption can also be applied by waiting and observing the offense's maneuvers, keeping the defensive line's cohesion. Steals are the best a defense can do, as they end the opponents' possession and shift the team from the defensive end to an attacking opportunity. Steals often can be the starting point for fast transitions. They can come in both ways. Pressing and thus grabbing the ball, forcing the opponents to make a turnover, or disrupting and being ready to exploit the opponents' turnovers due to their problematic and confused maneuvers.

Communication has been mentioned many times throughout and cannot be underestimated in its importance. Sometimes, a teammate nearer the ball carrier will turn towards this player, closing in for the tag and leaving a space behind them. It is at this point the next defender in line closes the gap and communicates to all players especially to the player that left the space in defense, that they have done so. This allows the pressing defender to confidently continue on with the job of making the tag on the ball carrier, knowing that the gap left behind them has now been closed. Along with this action, the other defenders also close any gaps that are created in the defensive line, again communicating that they have also closed the gaps. A simple term to use in this situation is yelling, "I have your back."

Techniques to Prevent Scoring

In touch rugby, preventing the opponent from scoring results from a combination of tactical positioning and defensive techniques. By pressing high and going for the touch early, adopting a proactive and not reactive stance, the defense can create problems for the attacking team's flow and force errors.

However, they must do this without losing their composure or leaving open spaces. As we said earlier, a defender who goes for the touch could be an opportunity for an offloading or a direction change and other moves that could result in a defensive gap and an opportunity to score for the opponent. This means the defenders should be careful not to leave the line open while pressing the ball carrier and instead retreat in time to maintain it.

We have also already mentioned the roles of the three positions, centers, wingers, and links, and how important it is to observe the opponent's game and communicate fast on who marks who and possible threats. We must add the "squeeze" defense scheme. In this scheme, there are three middle players as the team is defending instead of two. In this way, the defense creates a numerical advantage in the middle of the play against the two centers of the attacking team. This scheme was created because of the increasingly fast pace of touch rugby and the ability of more players to use the offensive techniques we've seen, such as changing rapidly the direction of the movement with a sidestep. Putting three middle defenders can help prevent frontal attacks. However, another problem is created since the wings become more open. That's why, in this defensive tactic, speed is crucial. When the center of the opponent passes the ball to a wing, the closest of the three defensive centers must run fast to cover the space where the player receives the pass.

Tagging Techniques and Practices

We have mentioned tagging and its importance several times so far, and it's clear that effective tagging is crucial for a good defensive function. If we want to be more precise, we'll say that there is not a strictly right or wrong tagging, though there are some things players should keep in mind. First and foremost, the tag must be executed swiftly and accurately, not leaving the chance for the attacker to evade the touch by offloading. On the other hand, the defender must be careful not to commit an overtly strong contact ending in a penalty. Also, avoid running so fast at the attacker that you make the tag but then overrun the place where the tag occurred, putting yourself even further offside, and instead of having to only run back 7 meters, having to run back 8/9 meters or even more.

Positioning is important for successfully tagging, so players must be careful to keep the right positions. The defending middles can touch a middle and stop their attacking move, and so on, with the links and the wings. Defenders must be careful in maintaining an advantageous position while considering the attacker's direction and speed. To practice effective and precise tagging, the team can work with some drills during training. One of them could be a mirror tag. In this drill, one player is designated as the tagger and another player as the mover. The tagger tries to mirror the movers' movements. This exercise helps with developing quick reactions and synchronizing the defenders' movements with those of the attackers. This is crucial to gain the advantage and be able to stop their attacking moves with the touch. We must keep in mind that the attacker always has the advantage of the initiative. This drill is very helpful to minimize that advantage and make defenders much more ready to react in time.

Another drill is putting out cones and making players move in a zig-zag pattern, quickly weaving through the cones laterally and changing directions. This is similar to what we've seen before for the offensive end. In the case of defense and touch, the exercises with cones can help improve lateral movements and sidesteps, which are crucial for following the ball carrier's movement and direction changes and maintaining balance. The tag is not made only by the hand—that's the conclusion—but by the leg and foot position, balance, and quick reaction of the whole body to the attacker's attempt.

Finally, a good method to prepare a team defensively and, in particular, for tagging successfully would be simulating real-game scenarios. This way, coaches can make the players practice tagging in several situations so they can be better prepared to face unpredictable and diverse situations in the confusion of the real game. A few examples would be set up two-on-one or three-on-two situations, where the defenders must find a way to act quickly and precisely, being at a disadvantage. Also, give some visual or auditory cues, such as signals and words, related especially to tagging, so the players can help each other and react faster to unpredictable movements of the opponents.

Deciphering the Opponents' Gameplay

Observing and studying the opponent team's gameplay is always very useful and, sometimes, can even be decisive. Who wouldn't want to know their opponents and how they play? There are some methods a coaching staff and the players could follow:

1. **Player-specific analysis:** This means identifying players with a leading role in the opponent team and who are playmakers or scorers. After that, it follows an in-depth analysis of those key opponent players' characteristics, strengths, weaknesses, and playing styles.

2. **Pattern recognition:** The second point is not about individual players but schemes the opponent coach uses or, more in general, patterns that, for whatever reason, systematically recur in the team's offensive movements. That can be made by analyzing positioning, player movements, and set-piece plays.

The reading of the opposition must be available to the team players at the practical level. In order to do so, a team must have some clues and signals that can convey information immediately about the opponent's moves and gameplay from the bench to the players or among them.

Keys to a Solid Defensive Line

We've already seen some important defensive aspects. Now we'll add some fundamental concepts about the team's solid defensive function.

- **Alignment:** Players should be attentive to maintaining proper spacing and keeping the defensive line, covering the width and the depth, reducing the possibility of leaving gaps and open spaces for the attackers to break through.

- **Applying pressure:** The defense must tend to apply consistent pressure to the offense, making it challenging for the attackers to execute plays and disrupting the game flow.

- **Adjusting positions and reacting quickly:** The defensive line should be proactive and not passive, reacting swiftly to the movements of the offense.

- **Anticipating the opponent:** The defense should try to anticipate the opponent's plays and not just follow their movements. To do so, it's important to observe and study the opponent, their body language, the patterns of their plays, and their touch rugby tactics.

- **Communication:** Nothing can work well if there is effective communication between the players, in this case, of the defensive line. Players should share quickly and precisely information about the opponents' moves and intentions, raising the collective understanding of their game and how it can be anticipated and disrupted. It is also paramount that the defensive line knows exactly what tag count they are on at all times.

We will talk again about defense in the following chapters.

Chapter 5:

Set Plays and Strategies

There is no I in TEAM. –Unknown

Adapting From Offense to Defense to Offense

The fast-paced nature of touch rugby and the continuous interplay between the attacking and defensive end require players to be able to shift gears fast. Adapting between offense and defense is crucial because touch rugby has a dynamic and fluid nature, and possessions can change with great speed. Players must be ready to adjust and change their stance from offensive to defensive and the opposite in no time.

Quick transitions from offense to defense and the opposite can help the team maintain momentum and sustain pressure on the opponent, thus offering a tactical advantage. When the individual players are capable of adapting fast from one end of the game to the other, the team will be more coordinated and ready to respond to any kind of situation faster. In a fast-paced game like touch rugby, a few seconds can decide an entire play and even the game.

If we want to identify some traits that can help with shifting gears, we will return to essential elements we've already seen, such as effective communication and solid defense. When the players communicate fast and use clear and concise verbal cues and signals, they can maintain the team's cohesion more easily in the case of rapid shifts. Also, defense is fundamental because if a team transitions to defense fast and focuses on offensive readiness, the game's momentum cannot be entirely lost, even if the offense does not work very well for a part of the game. Defense is key because it does not need a certain flow or rhythm like offense, but, rather, requires players to be prepared and focused on transitioning fast, making touches effectively, anticipating plays, and disrupting the opponent's flow and rhythm. Maintaining momentum, thanks to good communication and solid defense, helps a lot with transitioning to offense and creating flow with quick decision-making. We'll see more on that in the following paragraph.

Strategic Timing

Strategic timing is the well-calculated and precise execution of movements and actions by the players, i.e., being able to understand when the right time is to initiate plays and make touches in order to gain tactical advantage. Timing is really crucial for touch rugby, as the game is particularly fast-paced and has very few contacts, so split-second decisions can determine the outcome of a game.

We could say that timing is everything. From an offensive perspective, it enables players to exploit gaps in the defensive line, ensures that passes arrive at the receivers in optimal positions, and confuses defenders, as it consists of completing an action before the defense is set and prepared to deal with it.

From a defensive perspective, good timing prevents the attacking team from executing successful breaks, stopping them with well-timed touches. It anticipates passes, intercepting them and disrupting the offensive flow with timely defensive actions, forcing the opponents to reset or make mistakes, contributing to regaining possession.

And if all that sounds too abstract and generic and is making you think, "Yes, thank you very much; now how can we create timing?" the following points can help with the implementation, giving practical sense to theory:

1. Create simulation drills that replicate possible game scenarios during the training. The drills must focus on decision-making under pressure and constraints, pushing players to improve on-field timing.

2. Use the video analysis, which we will talk more about in the next chapter of the book. Analyzing moves and when they were successful or not can help players refine their sense of timing by watching themselves as external observers.

3. Implement reaction time training. Incorporating exercises that focus on developing quick decision-making and rapid response. This way, the players' overall responsiveness can improve substantially so that they can have good timing.

Timing is crucial in gaining a competitive edge on the touch rugby field, and teams can elevate their performance through targeted drills, working on reaction time training, and using video analysis.

Switching and the Cut Pass

When watching touch rugby, it is easy to note that the runners are standing uniformly, and the ball carrier moves sideways. This creates the conditions for switch passes and sham switch runs. Nevertheless, the effectiveness of these movements remains a topic of discussion among specialists. In the typical criticism, they are referred to as "lazy" assistants since they sometimes fail to provide good results that are proportionate to the amount of work that is put in.

In this context, the most important skills and strategies include the creation of overloads, which are situations with more attackers than defenders. Regarding switching passes, experts propose looping after the pass rather than depending on switch passes. The use of this tactical change guarantees that runners are not restricted by the limits of the switch, which in turn enables more dynamic attacking plays to be executed.

Having a solid understanding of when to carry out a switch pass is essential. The winger and their inside counterpart are the ones who should be responsible for this move. Through the implementation of this tactical decision, the ball is brought back into play, and the potential disadvantage of sprinting over the sideline is avoided, thus averting the unneeded loss of possession.

Player Width and Spacing

In touch rugby, players often adopt a certain fixed spacing, with each player keeping a position that is equal in distance from the previous player. This fixed spacing can give some predictability from a defensive standpoint, and it also restricts the diversity of rushing lines and overall offensive innovation.

So, this prescribed space is something that players are urged to move away from in order to increase their potential for attacking. In order to make the most of the whole width of the pitch, wings should position themselves in close proximity to the sideline. At the same time, other players should be aggressively adjusting their spacing in order to create an attacking shape that is more dynamic and unpredictable.

We have seen that touch rugby, which is well-known for its fast-paced and fun character, is often believed to be a quick method to start playing the game of rugby. Nevertheless, despite the fact that it is of the utmost importance to preserve its entertaining nature, there is value in incorporating basics that improve the overall level of play. Excellent execution and, eventually, a higher pleasure of the game are both outcomes that may be achieved via the application of patience, perseverance, and concentrated practice on the fundamentals. By embracing these foundations from the beginning of the season, you are laying the groundwork for a more sophisticated and pleasant game of touch rugby in the future.

Pump Fake

A pump fake in touch rugby is a communication technique. Its purpose is to indicate that a pass may not be the best choice at the time. Rather than making a dangerous pass, the player who is carrying the ball will perform a pump fake, which is a throwing action that seems like they are passing the ball. The message that is sent via the pump fake is that the player does not want to pass the ball in a certain direction at the moment in order to avoid turning it over.

In order for players to shift their posture and be ready for an alternate move, it is a signal that is universally recognized. When a pump fake is executed in touch rugby, the immediate reaction is to clear out. Immediately after a player has identified the pump fake, their objective is to rapidly leave the area where they were trying to get access to the open space. The action of moving quickly is referred to as "clearing out." The player not only prevents a possible turnover by departing the disputed area as quickly as possible, but they also provide possibilities for their teammates to take advantage of the space that has been freed up.

The most important idea that underpins these moves is the effective use of space. It is possible for a player to keep control of the ball without putting himself in danger of turnovers by doing a pump fake and clearing off the defender as quickly as possible if they find themselves in a situation where getting open is difficult. The players of the team are able to make intelligent maneuvers and generate opportunities for strong attacking plays as a result of the cleared space.

In order to effectively use these tactics, the players have to show that they are able to adapt to new circumstances and that they are aware of what's happening in the game at all times. The ability to identify the pump fake, comprehend the ramifications of the situation, and quickly respond by clearing out shows a high degree of game intelligence. In the game, these techniques are contingent on the coordinated effort of the team, in which players interact with one another to decrease the frequency of turnovers and enhance the number of options for offensive play. In touch rugby, the use of these methods enhances the game's possession-oriented gameplay, underlining the necessity of maintaining control and minimizing risks in order to obtain favorable outcomes in the game.

Chapter 6:

Conditioning for Touch Rugby

Rugby is a game that teaches you to seize opportunities and NEVER back down!

It doesn't matter whether you're a seasoned player or just starting out; in order to get the most out of your touch rugby experience, you need to work on improving essential parts of your game, such as your fitness, speed, and agility. The fact that touch rugby does not include tackles, scrums, or mauls may give the game a more relaxed atmosphere; nevertheless, this does not imply that players do not approach it with the same amount of passion and energy as other forms of rugby.

How to Take Your Game to the Next Level in Touch Rugby

Taking into consideration the following essential features will allow you to get the most out of your touch rugby experience:

1) **Putting fitness, speed, and agility at the forefront.** Training sessions should be performed on a regular basis in order to improve your endurance, stamina, and general fitness. Having a physique that is in good shape not only improves your performance but also lowers the likelihood that you will get an injury.

Develop your straight-line speed and agility in order to win races against other competitors. In order to ensure that your speed is not just track-worthy but also rugby-specific, you need to tailor your training to match the dynamic motions that are often observed during touch rugby.

Master the technique of quickly shifting directions in order to demonstrate agility. You should include agility workouts that simulate the unpredictability of touch rugby in order to improve your ability to navigate around opponents with dexterity.

2) **Training that is specific to touch rugby.** Make use of the RAMP approach, which stands for Range of Motion, Activation, Movement Preparation, and Potentiation, while doing structured warm-ups. The purpose of this individualized warm-up program is to prepare your body for the specific demands of touch rugby, which will allow you to play at your absolute best.

Include agility-focused exercises that are specifically designed for touch rugby as part of your speed training routine. Your capacity to traverse the field with accuracy may be improved via the use of exercises that focus on agility. Make agility a top priority by doing specific exercises like the T-Sprint, Zig Zag Sprints, and

Broken 100s. Your agility and reactivity will be improved via the use of these workouts, which imitate the fast changes in direction that are fundamental to touch rugby.

3) **Exercises that Build Strength and Power.** Although touch rugby may not need the same level of sheer strength as full-contact rugby, developing strength and power that is above average can improve your overall performance. Strength-building activities such as squats, box jumps, pull-ups, bench presses, and other exercises should be included in your gym training routine. To improve strength and power at home, you may make use of exercises that include your own bodyweight, programs that involve resistance bands, and improvised items such as boulders or sandbags.

4) It is imperative that you never undervalue the significance of a good cooldown. Devote some of your time to exercises such as reducing your pulse, static stretching, and foam rolling, an optional activity. This expedites the recuperation process, reduces the amount of muscular discomfort you experience, and prepares your body for the subsequent touch rugby practice.

Physical Requirements of Touch Rugby: A Comprehensive Guide

Touch rugby is a fast-paced version of rugby, as we've already said several times, and that means it requires a distinct set of physical components in order to negotiate the large playing field associated with the activity successfully. Touch rugby is a sport that combines characteristics such as cardiovascular endurance, speed, agility, and a touch of strength and power. Since there are only six players on each team on the field, there are many open spaces during the game, thus opportunities to run fast and move in various directions. So, besides all the rest, we should discuss the physical requirements that make touch rugby such an intriguing combination of athleticism.

One of the most important factors in sustained action is cardiovascular fitness. When it comes to touch rugby, cardiovascular fitness might be considered the most important factor. The critical aspect is your capacity to take in, transport, and make use of oxygen, and it is shown in your maximum oxygen consumption (VO_2 max).

Touch rugby requires a powerful cardiovascular system because of the lengthy durations of play that are combined with the little stoppages that occur throughout the game, as there are no timeouts or breaks, except for just a one-minute half break. The cardiovascular system, respiratory system, circulatory system, and muscles all work together to ensure that the flow of play is continuous. Players who do not have sufficient cardiovascular fitness run the danger of being sidelined, struggling to catch their breath, and being unable to make a contribution that is relevant to the game.

The importance of speed in open spaces cannot be overstated. Touch rugby is characterized by more open spaces than other team sports, which makes speed an essential component of physical conditioning. It is possible that the capacity to cover terrain quickly, whether in offensive or defensive maneuvers, might be the deciding element in determining whether or not that move is successful.

However, touch rugby, in contrast to sprinting, requires players to have multidirectional speed, meaning they must accelerate, decelerate, and reaccelerate in order to play the game. The ability to change speed with such agility not only improves evasiveness but also makes athletes more difficult to touch. Sprint endurance is also very important since it ensures that athletes are able to maintain their speed for the whole of the team's competition.

Furthermore, mobility, or the ability to react quickly to stimuli, is extremely important. Touch rugby requires agile footwork and fast directional shifts, in contrast to full-contact traditional rugby, which may compensate for agility via the sport's emphasis on muscle. When it comes to achieving success on the touch rugby field, though, it is essential to be able to avoid collisions with other players and quickly adjust your strategy in reaction to the ebb and flow of the game.

We said that muscle is not as important for touch rugby as in traditional rugby. Yet, strength and power continue to be important factors in touch rugby despite the fact that it is not a full-contact sport. It is not necessary for players to have the same level of muscle mass as in the traditional versions of rugby however, having a foundation of strength and power is beneficial to overall performance. Moreover, these fitness components make a beneficial contribution to the development of speed, agility, and joint stability. Touch rugby players may achieve a balance between quickness and the resilience necessary to resist the demands of the game by including some strength training in their training schemes. This can be accomplished with as few as a couple of gym sessions per week.

Touch rugby is a diverse sport that combines accuracy and athleticism. In order to be ready and successful, players must adapt their fitness to suit the requirements of the sport. Having enough strength and power gives resilience to the touch rugby adventure while having cardiovascular endurance feeds continuous action, speed gives a chance to exploit wide spaces, agility defines rapid reactions, and a touch of agility defines swift replies. We can say that it is a symphony of many aspects of fitness that come together to create the excitement of the game. It is more than just the basic moves of the game that matter.

Exercises to Foster Speed and Agility

We've said that touch rugby requires more than just the ability to run in a straight path; it also requires agility, which is the necessary skill to change directions quickly. Speed alone is not enough in touch rugby; players need to have the agility to quickly change direction, avoid opponents, and execute precise plays on the field. Even the slightest contact counts as a tackle, so agility, which is defined as the ability to regulate and maneuver speed efficiently, is a differentiating factor. Here are some specific routines you can include in your training in order to improve your agility and take your performance to the next level:

- **Catch me if you can.** Place obstacles in the center of a square that is ten meters in measurement. The participants take turns running around the exterior of the building or through the obstacles. The first player to reach the opposing corner wins. Perform three to five sets, pausing for two to three minutes in between each set.

- **Rolling start acceleration.** Put markers at ten, fifteen, and twenty meters. You should begin by jogging to the starting line, then accelerate to 10 meters, then slow down to 15 meters, and then accelerate once more to 20 meters. Make your way back to the beginning. Perform three to five sets, pausing for two to three minutes in between each set.

- **Standing start acceleration.** In a manner comparable to the rolling beginnings, but with each attempt beginning from a standing standpoint. In addition to accelerating and changing directions (backward or forward). Markers at five meters, ten meters, and fifteen meters. Sprint ahead, backward, then forward while progressively slowing down. This should be done while in a prone or supine posture. Between each set, switch the starting locations. Perform three to five sets, pausing for two to three minutes in between each set.

- **Acceleration and turning to the left or right.** There is a marker at ten meters, and there are two markings five meters to the left and right. You should run to the 10-meter marker, then make a cut to the left or right, and then speed up to the next marker. Continue moving forward despite the shift in direction. Repeat for three to five sets, pausing for two to three minutes in between each set.

- **Medley of sprints.** Improves your ability to sprint over short, medium, and long distances. Sprints of 10 times 15 meters, 8 times 25 meters, 6 times 40 meters, and 4 times 70 meters. In between sprints, you should walk back and recuperate as necessary.

- **A rapid-fire medley of rugby pitches.** Performing flying starts and pick-ups, sprinting and backpedaling, measuring lengths and widths, and suicides on the rugby field. Participate in a number of different sprint disciplines in order to improve your speed across all distances.

- **T-sprint.** In a T-shaped formation, place four marker cones five meters away from one another. Begin by sprinting forward, then sidestepping to the right, then moving over to the left cone, then sidestepping back to the center, and finally running backward to the beginning position. Additionally, add an agility requirement by touching each cone as you repeat. In between each set, take a minute or two to rest off.

- **The T grid sprint.** Remember to use the T-shaped grid that was used in the last exercise. While you are focusing on turning off both sides, you should sprint around the outside of the T. This workout will help you improve your agility as well as your ability to turn.

- **Zig-zag sprints.** Place 10 marker cones 2-3 meters apart from one another. Sprint past the cones in a zigzag pattern while starting from a rolling start location of five meters. Concentrate on jogging in a straight path while dynamically pushing off of the foot that is on the outer. Sprint out to a final marker that is around ten to fifteen meters away from the last cone.

- **Broken 100s.** In a location that is twenty meters in size, establish a marker configuration. In a continuous manner, run out and return to each of the markers. Repeat after a brief rest of sixty to ninety seconds. Improve both the quality and quantity of your sprinting by doing numerous sets and taking longer pauses.

Unlocking of Strength and Power

Because there are no bone-crushing tackles or violent scrums in touch rugby, some people may be led to assume that strength and power are secondary. On the contrary, developing strength and power that are above average may considerably improve your performance in touch rugby. We will investigate the reasons why these characteristics are important, as well as examine two complete exercises that are meant to improve your performance.

Strength is the cornerstone of prowess in athletic abilities. The creation of force, regardless of speed, is what we mean when we talk about strength, and it is the foundation upon which many other athletic pursuits are built. In touch rugby, having a strong foundation of strength gives various advantages. For the purpose of outmaneuvering opponents on the field, having powerful musculature is essential since it adds to quicker sprints and more agile movements.

One major benefit of strength is that it gives stability to the joints Strong muscles serve a crucial role in maintaining good joint alignment, which in turn reduces the risk of injuries linked with sudden changes in direction.

Power is the ability to unleash speed at every turn. When it comes to touch rugby, power may help you play at a higher level as it enables explosive movements, which in turn result in greater leaps and quicker sprints, which are crucial for both offensive and defensive plays. The ability to change directions quickly is a trademark of a skilled touch rugby player. Increasing this ability via power training makes it possible to make smooth transitions and responses when playing on the field.

The Development of Strength and Power Training Routines for Touch Rugby

In spite of the fact that the gym is the perfect location for strength and power training, it is also possible to design effective exercises that can be performed in the comfort of one's own kitchen. Listed below are two full exercises that may be performed in a gym to improve your performance in touch rugby.

First workout:

- Squats: four sets of eight repetitions each.

- Box Jumps: Four sets of ten repetitions each.

- 3 sets of pull-ups, with the maximum number of repetitions.

- Bench Press: three sets of eight repetitions each.

- Performing three sets of push-ups.

- Swing with a single arm: three sets of twelve repetitions for each arm.

Second workout:

- Perform four sets of eight repetitions for the deadlift.

- Perform four sets of ten repetitions for the broad jump.

- Performing three sets of pulldowns (to maximum repetitions)

- 3 sets of 8 repetitions for the dumbbell shoulder press.

- Three sets of barbell push-presses (to maximum repetitions) are required.

- Rows from a seated position: three sets of twelve repetitions for each arm.

- Revolving medical practice ball throws. Three sets of twelve repetitions each.

Additionally, there are a variety of home-friendly options that may help people build strength and power, even if they do not have access to a gym:

- Performing push-ups.

- Performing pull-ups.

- Stretching using a resistance band.

- The use of hops and two-footed leaps to achieve height or distance.

- Lifting rocks, barrels, or sandbags.

- Squats, lunges, and step-ups on your own body weight.

- Performing Chinese planks and hip raises.

- Every single core workout using just your own body weight.

You should consider including some of these exercises in your training routine, making sure to balance them out with sessions that focus on fitness, speed, and agility. You will be able to enhance your performance in touch rugby by devoting a few hours every week. This will allow you to reduce the likelihood of any injuries occurring and demonstrate your newly acquired strength and power on the field.

The Art of Warming Up

If you want to get the most out of any game or training session, you need to do more than simply get right into the action; you need to warm up in a way that is deliberate and intentional. The act of warming up is not only a routine; rather, it is an essential component in effectively maximizing performance and minimizing the likelihood of damage. In touch rugby, where dynamic movements and explosive actions are the norm, a warm-up that is well-structured is your passport to a session that is both safer and more productive. We are going to get into the subtleties of the RAMP approach, which, as a reminder, stands for Range of motion, Activation, Movement preparation, and Potentiation. This strategy is designed to maximize the effectiveness of your touch rugby warm-up.

First is dynamic flexibility for peak performance, which is referred to as the range of motion. There has been a shift away from static stretches and toward dynamic stretches, which serve the dual goal of extending muscles and priming the cardiovascular system. Static stretches have been relegated to the background. The execution of dynamic stretches helps to keep the heart rate up and raises the core temperature, which in turn prepares the body for maximum performance. Squats that range from shallow to deep, walking lunges with overhead reaches, and high knee jogging are some examples of dynamic stretches that may help improve flexibility and preparedness. In order to get a more effective warm-up, it is recommended that you forego the conventional static stretches and instead focus on the vigorous range of motion exercises.

In the second step, activation, essential muscles for rugby rigors are awoken. Sitting for long periods of time or commuting might cause important muscle groups to go into a state of dormancy. The glutes, core, and upper back are some of the muscles that are targeted by activation exercises, which are beneficial since they guarantee that these muscles are prepared for the dynamic demands of touch rugby. By doing these workouts, which include brief contractions at around twenty percent of the maximum effort, you may wake up muscles that have been inactive without depleting them. It is important to include exercises such as one-leg standing with quadricep extensions, abdominal "snap" bracing, and band pull-aparts in order to engage critical muscle groups and set the scene for the best performance.

Third, movement preparation involves imitating future actions in order to ensure smooth transitions. When it comes to the movement preparation phase, it is beneficial to engage in activities that are similar to the future movements but on a simpler level. The objective is to synchronize your technique, which will ensure consistency even while working with lesser weights. This may be accomplished by doing bodyweight squats before barbell squats or strides before sprints. During this period of preparation, you should practice in the same manner as you want to perform, making sure to keep the same form and accuracy.

Fourth is potentiation. The culmination of your warm-up is the potentiation stage, which is designed to maximize the efficiency with which your muscles fire and the amount of power that is produced. Squat jumps, push-ups, and sprints are examples of the kinds of explosive activities that make up the optimal arsenal for potentiation. Not only will these workouts have your muscles working hard, but they will also get your neurological system ready for maximum performance capabilities. At the conclusion of the warm-up, you should experience a rush in strength and power, and you should be completely ready to perform at your highest level in the next game or training session.

Keep in mind that the length of time you spend warming up is a matter of personal preference. Adapt it to your age, the amount of exercise you do, and any other special needs. It is possible that a more active routine may need a shorter warm-up, while a more sedentary lifestyle or any current pain may call for a lengthier warm-up. Assuring that your warm-up is tailored to your unique needs guarantees an effective and targeted preparation for the touch rugby trip that lies ahead. When it comes to the complicated dance that is touch rugby, the warm-up is your overture; if you set the stage correctly, the performance will follow suit.

The Importance of an Adequate Cool Down

After a session of intensive touch rugby, it may be tempting to skip the cooldown and go directly to the showers. This is because the adrenaline of the workout provides a lot of energy. On the other hand, if you ignore this essential component of your workout program, it may slow down your recovery and prevent you from making progress in the future. Let's investigate the reasons why a well-structured cooldown is necessary, and then we'll break down the important components that should be included in your post-workout routine.

As is the case with other sports, touch rugby exerts a significant amount of strain on your body. Muscles that are contracted, heart rates that are higher, and an increase in the creation of lactic acid are all reactions that occur as a result of stress. The right cooldown acts as a transitional phase between the strenuous exercise you just completed and the crucial recovery period that follows. A cooldown helps you recover more quickly by encouraging a gradual return to the condition you were in before you started exercising. This reduces the amount of muscular pain you experience and gets your body ready for the next training session. A full cooldown that takes just 10 minutes to complete delivers various advantages, including:

- Promoting a quicker recovery by restoring the homeostasis of your body, which is referred to as "accelerated recovery."

- Reduction in muscle soreness. This helps alleviate post-exercise soreness and tightness, which are typical complaints among touch rugby players.

- The ability to counteract adaptive shortening results in improved flexibility, which in turn reduces the risk of injury and improves overall flexibility.

- Release of tension. Foam rolling is an effective method for releasing tension in the muscles and developing mobility.

In conclusion, the additional minutes that are spent on a good cooldown are not at all amounts of time that are squandered. On the contrary, they are an investment in your future performance and progression, guaranteeing that you continue to be nimble, resistant to injuries, and prepared for the next spectacular touch rugby practice.

Chapter 7:

Mental Aspects of the Game

Rugby is like war! Easy to start, difficult to stop, and impossible to forget!

Good physical condition and skills are essential in touch rugby, but so is being mentally prepared and strong. In the following paragraphs, we'll talk about game awareness, reading your team and the opposing team, and being mentally tough and motivated. The mental aspects are sometimes overlooked because they can feel abstract, and while everybody understands the importance of being athletic and skilled, some do not pay attention to the mental part of the game. Players and teams must avoid this mistake that could literally ruin their efforts and ambitions. Being mentally prepared and strong can instead multiply the players and the team's strengths and help them overcome their weaknesses.

Game Awareness

Being game-aware means being mentally focused and ready to engage in the game's dynamics. Here are five tips to help players achieve game awareness:

1. First and foremost, players must be sure to know all the rules of the game and the tactics of their teams. You can't even play the game without this knowledge, let alone being mentally aware. Game awareness is, first of all, understanding the game and your team's plans.

2. Mental readiness is crucial for game awareness, but it depends on the individuals, and there isn't a specific way everybody should follow to achieve it. It's up to the players to engage in pre-game rituals or routines that help them transition into the right mindset. Some techniques one could try are visualization exercises, deep breathing, or just listening to motivational music. Every player can find what drives them and create a mental pre-game routine to signal to the brain that it's time to shift into game mode. There could also be a team pre-game routine if the players and coaches agree it helps them collectively.

3. Having a positive mindset and feeling confident can help with game awareness. Players should approach challenges and setbacks with resilience and optimism, as it boosts individual performance and also contributes to a cohesive and supportive team environment. On the other hand, entering the game with a negative mindset can create confusion and

panic, which is disconnection, the opposite of game awareness.

4. Focusing on the present moment is essential for game awareness. Players should not despair of past mistakes or worry about what will happen. The point is to stay focused on the current play so they can respond quickly and effectively, maximizing their impact on the game.

5. Ultimately, game awareness is not a mind trick, but it depends on the ability to adapt to changing circumstances and not lose composure. Being prepared for momentum changes, difficult situations, and the need to adapt their style means staying in the game. It all comes down to practice, exercise, teamwork.

Reading Your Teammates

Reading your teammates means being able to understand their intentions and their emotional stance in the game quickly, which is beyond knowing their individual playing styles. Reading your teammates can be achieved through the following techniques:

1. **Knowing their body language.** By observing your teammate's posture, gestures, and facial

expressions, you can grasp if they feel confident and excited or frustrated and deluded at a certain moment of the game. This can come naturally, especially after playing with people on the same team for a while, yet it demands an effort and the will to understand and care about others' emotions.

2. **Understanding their emotional states.** Following point one, being able to really get your teammates' emotional state can help gauge their motivation and resilience. Players must support and encourage each other or flow with momentum and excitement when things are going well.

3. **Understanding their verbal communication.** Different characters have different ways to express emotions. Some touch rugby players can be more silent and focused, trying to lead by example and determination, while others are more vocal, trying to encourage and give directions. Knowing their way can make you understand more than they say. It is also important to be open when a certain style gives you problems.

4. **Using non-verbal signals and eye contact.** With quick glances, nods, and hand gestures, teammates can convey instant messages to

each other during the game and indicate planned set-piece plays. When players establish similar cues, they can make split-second decisions and coordinate their games more easily and effectively.

5. **Knowing their playing patterns.** When a player knows how their teammates move in the field and which positions and plays they prefer or do best, they can make the best out of it for themselves by taking advantageous positions, being prepared for the next move, and creating spaces and opportunities for themselves or other teammates.

Reading your teammates offers essential benefits to a player and the team. It enhances coordination, allows quick decision-making, builds trust, and makes the players and the team more capable of adapting to changing situations. All these elements are crucial for the team to cooperate better and be more versatile and resilient.

Reading the Opposition

Reading the opposition in touch rugby, like in other sports, is equally important to knowing your teammates. Understanding their strengths and weaknesses is the basis of every team tactic and individual play if it is to be successful. Here are some techniques that can help with reading the opponent:

1. **Noticing individual players' weaknesses.** Every team is made of individual players, and their weaknesses are the more obvious and manifest weaknesses of the team.

2. **Observing the players' positioning and movement patterns.** This can help the team understand their tactics and counteract them anticipating their plays. The first things to watch are the positions and the preferred areas of the key players and how they move off the ball.

3. **Understand their team style.** The coaching staff should have a clear image of the opponent's basic tactics and overall style of play, be it more offensive, defensive, fast-paced, or more controlled, and explain it to the players.

4. **Understand their strategies and tactics.** Analyzing the set-piece tactics of the opponent allows the team to anticipate plays and organize effective countermeasures, both in offense and defense.

Knowing the opponent's strengths and weaknesses is the basis for planning the team's tactics for the precise game. Of course, every touch rugby team has standard plays and tactics of their own, and some coaches do not want to adapt to the opponent's game, but that's practically impossible. You need to have a view of the opposition's game and, one way or another, adapt to it if you want to raise the possibility of winning. No plan can bring victory on its own since it will collide with the opponent's plans. Being able to adapt formations and schemes can secure an advantage over the opposition in the defending and offensive end of the field.

To be more precise, we should say that identifying weaknesses can create opportunities by directing attacks toward the gaps, exploiting the opponent's vulnerabilities, such as not-so-solid defending players. On the other side, knowing attacking tactics and the best players of the opposition can help make it more difficult for them to find their way to your try line by blocking the plays and putting more players on their best attackers.

Mental Toughness

Although the phrase "mental toughness" is often used in the sports industry, athletes—especially young ones—may find it difficult to understand what it really means. Parents and coaches alike often stress the need for mental toughness, but it's not always obvious how to cultivate this kind of thinking. Many coaches look for players who already possess mental toughness, believing it to be an innate trait rather than deliberately encouraging its development. But just like any other talent, mental toughness can and should be developed; the sooner this process starts, the better.

Building mental toughness in young athletes entails developing certain traits that support a positive outlook. A robust mind has many different characteristics, but simplicity is essential, particularly when dealing with young people. Two essential qualities that are the cornerstones of mental toughness in young athletes are self-assurance and the capacity for accurate performance evaluation.

An essential component of mental toughness is self-assurance. A strong mentality arises from a strong sense of self-worth, and building self-assurance is a crucial life skill for young athletes. But cultivating true self-confidence is a complicated process. Though well-intentioned, traditional ways of rewarding young players for their accomplishments sometimes associate confidence with tangible results. It is essential to encourage young athletes to develop real self-confidence from within, based on an intrinsic conviction in their talents and abilities.

A useful practice for boosting self-esteem is helping young athletes modify their inner monologue. This three-step activity promotes a constructive change in their mental processes:

Step 1: Recognize and enumerate every negative term or doubt that they are now using in their self-talk.

Step 2: Create a list of encouraging and constructive phrases to counter the negative ideas you've uncovered.

Step 3: To strengthen a constructive self-dialogue, repeat the affirmations in a positive and constructive manner every day.

This simple but effective activity gives young athletes the tools to recognize how their words affect their self-confidence and offers a practical plan for developing a positive outlook.

In summary, mental toughness is a trainable talent that may be developed from an early age rather than an elusive trait reserved for a chosen few. Young athletes build a strong and resilient mentality by honing the skill of positive performance evaluation and emphasizing self-confidence. It is crucial for coaches and mentors to understand the value of developing mental toughness in young athletes and giving them the resources they need to handle the psychological components of touch rugby.

Goal-Setting and Visualization: The Powerful Pair for Sports Excellence

Making a clear mental image of the intended result is known as visualization or mental imagery. There are several convincing reasons why athletes practice visualization.

- **Improved performance:** By acting as a mental warm-up, visualization helps athletes experience success in advance. Athletes prepare their bodies and brains for optimal performance when the time comes by visualizing faultless execution.

- **Stress reduction:** Visualization is a technique for overcoming obstacles as well as achieving success. Athletes learn to overcome challenges and handle pressure gracefully in their minds, which helps them feel less nervous and stressed out during competition.

- **Skill refinement:** Mental imagery is not limited to performance in general; it can also be used to hone certain talents. Without putting in any physical effort, athletes may mentally rehearse complex maneuvers to refine their skills.

Having a successful image in your mind gives you more confidence. Athletes develop a strong sense of self-worth as they consistently see themselves accomplishing their objectives; this self-worth is crucial for handling the stresses of competition.

What Benefits Can Athletes Gain From Creating Goals?

Establishing goals gives athletes direction, drive, and a sense of purpose on their path. This is the reason why goal-setting is essential.

- **Purpose clarity:** Athletes may clearly sketch out their desired path by setting goals. Setting objectives gives you a concrete destination, whether you're going for skill mastery, personal best, or championship title.

- **Motivational catalyst:** Objectives are strong inducers of the inner drive required for intense practice and consistent effort. The pursuit of a well-defined objective drives athletes through obstacles and failures.

- **Measurable development:** Athletes may monitor their development by setting goals that serve as quantifiable benchmarks. Small victories along the way to a bigger objective provide encouragement and support for persistent hard work.

- **Focus and dedication:** Goal-oriented athletes have more dedication and focus. All actions, including lifestyle decisions and exercise regimens, align with the overall goals to maximize effectiveness and efficiency.

The advantages of goal-setting and visualization for athletes are as follows.

- **Enhanced performance:** By directing both mental and physical attention on a single goal, the combination of goal-setting and visualization improves performance as a whole.

- **Resilience in adversity:** Equipped with a defined aim and mental picture, touch rugby players overcome obstacles with fortitude. They see obstacles as opportunities rather than as barriers.

- **Enhanced confidence:** Setting goals gives you a feeling of direction, and visualization gives you steadfast confidence. When combined, they provide a powerful concoction that gives athletes the confidence to take on any competitive environment.

- **Optimized training:** Establishing goals ensures that training plans have a purpose and are suited to certain goals. During off-field preparations, visualization helps by mentally honing tactics and plans.

Essentially, the combination of goal-setting and visualization is a game-changer in the touch rugby world, revealing the full potential that every athlete has. Athletes who use their thoughts to visualize success and set lofty objectives not only improve their performance but also start a path of ongoing development and accomplishment.

Chapter 8:

Advanced Tactics and Strategies

If you can't out play them, then outwork them!

We have seen in previous chapters how important it is for a team to read its opponents' game and identify strengths and weaknesses in order to become more effective and impose its own plans. In this chapter, we will see some more specific tactical schemes for both the offense and the defense.

Attacking Plays: Concepts and Ideas for the Offense

First of all, we will see some very important concepts that are necessary to know in order to build the team's strategic plans. Gaining proficiency in these core attacking phrases prepares you for a coherent and successful offensive approach. The more players absorb these ideas, the more naturally they make judgments on the pitch, which helps create a dynamic and well-coordinated offensive team.

1. **Plant:** The ball carrier positions their hips and shoulders to face the try line in this method, which is executed at a critical juncture after being touched or making contact. After that, they set the ball down on the ground and walked all the way over it. The attack's subsequent stages are built up by this move.

2. **Ruck Area:** The space where the ball has been grounded after the plant is known as the ruck area. This is an important zone because, from here, the referee draws the 7-meter defensive line. The success of future offensive actions is typically determined by the dynamics inside the ruck region.

3. **Mark:** A place on the pitch that the referee designates for doing certain actions, such as planting or tapping. A player must position the ball exactly on the mark after being touched. In addition, players must ask the referee for the mark after a penalty or turnover before beginning to tap or plant.

4. **Yards/30s:** A strategic move in which the attacking team purposefully sprints straight toward the defense in an attempt to get touched. This play usually happens in the first three touches. This methodical procedure, with the dummy half placed thoughtfully,

allows for speedy plantings. Yards or 30s are essential in order to disrupt the defense and provide opportunities for focused assaults in later touches.

5. **Split:** A quick move in which the attacker plants the ball perfectly after starting a touch, then steps one step forward and one step back. By moving them to the back of the dummy half, they allow for a quick transfer from the dummy half to the planter who has completed the split.

6. **Peel:** A tactical move in which the player circles behind the receiver they just handed the ball to after passing it from the fake half. Running straight, the receiver turns into an outside support player. The peel gives the assault a degree of unpredictability that opens up big play possibilities.

Now we can pass to specific attacking tactical schemes and plays.

- **Pay attention to the referee:** One of the often disregarded elements of successful gaming is paying close attention to the referee in the middle of the heart-pounding action. In addition to serving as objective arbiters, referees may provide helpful coaching advice during play. The players should pay attention to the referee's orders, as they may include subtle clues and strategic advice that can change the game's direction.

- **Run straight with the ball:** An effective offense depends on making the most of every moment of control of the ball, which is a valuable resource. Players are instructed to run straight with the ball during touches 1–5. This methodical technique accomplishes two goals: it optimizes the use of all six touches and establishes the foundation for the attack's later stages.

- **Controlled approach to contact:** It is advised that players take a deliberate pause as they get closer to the contact area. When the ball is touched, this intentional slowdown enables instantaneous placement of the ball. Players have a critical advantage in establishing the cadence of the offensive sequence by guaranteeing a regulated and prompt reaction to contact.

- **Effective dummy half presence:** The effectiveness of the dummy half is critical to a well-planned assault. A fundamental idea is to have a dummy half placed such that, within a second or two after the ball is planted, it may be picked up. This smooth transition keeps the assault going and avoids any hiccups that may offer the opponent a defensive advantage.

- **Receiver movement:** The movement of the dummy half-pass receiver is the last component of the jigsaw. The receiver has to be moving even before they receive the ball in order to maximize this play. The receiver's prearranged location, which places them 2 meters to the side and 4 meters behind the "Ruck Area," guarantees that they are prepared to take advantage of the ball's delivery, adding to the attack's fluidity and dynamism.

- **Two-handed ball control:** In touch rugby, it is a tactical decision to hold the ball with two hands in order to confuse the opposing defense. Players create a dynamic scenario that challenges defenders and creates opportunities for smart attacking moves by maintaining control of the ball in an unexpected manner.

- **Ruck setup and purposeful touches:** In touch rugby, strategic touches may be an effective tool. Intentionally being touched has two benefits: it creates a ruck and forces the defenders to back off by seven meters. The deliberate use of the touch-and-retreat tactic throws off the defensive alignment and gives the attacking side favorable circumstances.

- **Initiative via player initiation:** One of the most important components of offensive strategy is controlling the game's tempo. The attacking side gains the ability to control the game's pace when they make contact with the defense. This control factor influences the attack's trajectory by enabling deliberate decision-making and strategic placement.

- **Dynamic dummy half play:** The dummy half plays a crucial part in planning the assault, and when they play dynamically, they may really affect the game. Setting up a complex play involves executing a dummy half throw to a receiver who is angling back to the ruck. More throwing possibilities are offered when the dummy half circles around behind the receiver in an attempt to take advantage of defensive weaknesses and maybe create an overlap.

- **Strategic substitution:** When your team has the ball on touches 1-3, strategic substitution turns into a tactical factor. A smooth transition is ensured by thoughtful subbing, where three players are ready to move the ball forward when a change is made. In addition to maximizing player energy, this tactical rotation supports a persistent and exciting attacking effort.

- **Tactical awareness via jersey numbers:** During the complex touch rugby dance, each attacker has to be able to read the jersey numbers of teammates who are in close proximity. This increased awareness makes it possible to make decisions quickly, which facilitates smooth coordination and improves the attacking moves of the team as a whole.

- **Even field spread for defensive disarray:** A well-thought-out field spread may be a powerful tool for severing the defense. By keeping the field evenly spaced, the opponent is forced to stretch their defensive covering, which widens the holes in their line. This deliberate dispersal creates the conditions for taking advantage of defensive weaknesses and winning calculated offensive plays.

- **Slanted runs for seamless passes:** In touch rugby, making accurate passes is an art form. Ball carriers and receivers may increase the impact of these plays by running slanted runs. In addition to making passes simpler, starting wide apart and sprinting on angles adds an element of unpredictability that keeps the defenders guessing.

- **Strategic positioning for dummy half runs:** To maximize the dummy half's participation while running directly at the defense, careful preparation is necessary. Ball carriers must see the dummy half's location before starting a run in order to strategically position themselves to reduce the amount of ground the dummy half must travel in order to make the pass. This synergy is further strengthened by effective communication, where words like "Down for you," "Grass," or "Pick me up" indicate a planned plant for the dummy half.

- **Dynamic support player contributions:** Similar to ball carriers in their ability to cause uncertainty, support players are sometimes the hidden stars of the offensive lineup. Support players become essential to the attacking plan by shifting their positions, requesting the ball, and staying at the right depth. Their dynamic contributions provide the team assault additional levels of intricacy, which makes it difficult for the opposition to anticipate and counter defensive maneuvers.

Defensive Plays: Neutralizing the Opposition

Proactive decision-making is important to dictate the game's pace and control the rhythm, neutralizing the opposition. Effective tagging is one of the primary ways to neutralize the opposition, as we saw earlier. Touches made accurately and efficiently disrupt the flow of the opponents' attacks by forcing them to reset and eventually lose possession. Defensive pressure forces turnovers and, again, disrupts the attacking team's flow, and strategic timing can anticipate plays and intercept passes.

But let's talk about some more specific and advanced tactical schemes for the defense. By implementing the following tactics, a team can create a robust defensive structure, limit the opponents' options, and regain possession:

- **Organize the defense into two distinct lines.** This structure makes it more difficult for the attacking team to find and exploit potential gaps in the initial phase of the attack.

- **Single-player rush.** After the tap (kick-off), only one player is designated to advance, so a full push due to the mandatory seven-meter retreat does not happen, and the defensive integrity is maintained for the subsequent phases.

- **Single defensive line.** The defensive line creates a united front and pressures the attacking team by moving up together. After the touch, the defensive line retreats swiftly and expects the second phase of the attack.

- **The drift defense.** This strategy focuses on shutting down wide channels effectively. The defenders move laterally to restrict the opponents' options as they attack and prevent them from gaining ground, moving the ball towards the try line. For the drift defense to work, there must be trust among defenders. This scheme relies on communication and certainty that the inside defender will cover the outside shoulder. It's all about cohesion.

- **Force attacks inside.** This is a more aggressive version of the drift scheme. This defensive tactic channels the opposing team's offensive play toward the center of the field. It's like trapping them, as the defensive wings can then close on the attackers in the middle and leave them with very limited options. This tactic can be particularly effective in touch rugby also because the playing area is relatively confined, and pushing the offense towards the center can result in a more manageable situation for the defense.

- **The box defense.** The other side of the coin to forcing the attacks inside, the box defense focuses on closing the corridors to the try line, keeping the line compact and solid, and intentionally leaving wide spaces on the edges. With this scheme, the defense compels the attackers to pass the ball to the edges and execute wide plays, creating the opportunity to intercept the ball and regain possession.

Chapter 9:

Game Analysis and Improvement

When your legs get tired, run with your heart!

The world of sports evolves constantly, and so do science and technology. In recent years, digital technology has emerged as a game-changer in sports, presenting the potential for growth that has never been seen before. Video analysis is one example of a technological innovation that is creating waves. This technology, which a few decades ago didn't exist and then was only available to professional teams, has now become an essential component even of junior sports. Because of the increased availability of software and camera systems in which teams recognize their strengths, define their deficiencies, and formulate strategies for improved performance, it is transforming.

Touch rugby teams can also benefit from those new technologies, using camera systems to gather insights into their games, which is helping to nurture the development of tactical thinking.

The objective measurement of performance in touch rugby players is achieved via video analysis, which provides coaches with an objective perspective broader than the one they can have by watching the game from the bench. Video analysis software gives an accurate picture of plays, wins, and losses, which improves the quality of feedback and coaching tactics based on the information provided.

Video performance analysis provides immediate and rapid feedback, which can help players grow. The evaluation of performance may be facilitated by the use of video analysis and artificial intelligence software within a few hours after each game, which enables players to make modifications from week to week. A player's motivation is fueled when they see actual outcomes, which is why progress tracking is important. The use of video analysis not only helps players develop from one game to the next, but it also gives a permanent record of how far they have come over the season.

Apart from individual progress, video analysis can help enhance the chemistry of a touch rugby team. Studying game videos as a group helps to strengthen both communication and teamwork. Participants are able to obtain an understanding of how their individual accomplishments affect the team, which in turn encourages them to engage in intensive training.

To better understand why sports video analysis is becoming an essential component of coaching approaches, let's go further into the causes behind this trend.

1. **Show, don't tell, and cater to those who learn best via visuals:** A remarkable sixty-

five percent of the world's population is a visual learner, meaning that they are able to take in knowledge more efficiently via the use of visual cues. There is a possibility that coaches who depend entirely on verbal communication may discover that the majority of their squad does not believe their messages to be meaningful. Enter the analysis of videos. Coaches trigger instantaneous understanding via the use of video clips, which are used to demonstrate both achievements and failures. This is a "light bulb moment" that goes beyond the scope of spoken education. Applications like Nacsport make this process more efficient by enabling coaches to annotate videos, add text, and arrange material in order to communicate in a manner that is both clear and succinct.

2. **Real-time response for adjustments made during the game:** Having the capability to deliver feedback in real-time while a match is in progress is a game-changer. When coaches use sophisticated software, they are able to share live statistic dashboards with the bench, which enables them to make modifications on the fly. The capacity can expand to include the sharing of video clips for the purpose of quick mistake review. The coaches have a strategic edge because of this quick feedback loop,

which enables them to make adjustments to their formations and strategies on the basis of the situation.

3. **Non-biased evaluation of criticism:** Criticism is not something that everyone reacts well to, and there are many players who are averse to input. An objective third party is brought into the equation via the use of video analysis, which eliminates any opportunity for subjective interpretations or disagreements. Whether it was a mistake in strategy or a momentary slip in focus, the film does not sugarcoat the truth. It is possible for coaches to conduct objective evaluations of player performance, identifying areas in which players may improve and recognizing triumphs. Because it places more of an emphasis on facts than on opinions, this objective approach helps to cultivate a more positive coach-player interaction.

4. **The strategy and scouting that give you power over your rivals:** The use of sports video analysis is not limited to the purpose of self-improvement; rather, it is a powerful instrument for analyzing and outsmarting competitors. The ability to scout other teams allows coaches to find vulnerabilities that may be exploited and strengths that can be

countered. It is possible to combine platforms such as Nacsport with external data sources in a smooth manner, which provides a full perspective of the playing style of the opponent. This strategic edge goes beyond the current squad, offering information that might impact training sessions and game planning. Generally speaking, this advantage is advantageous.

5. **Increasing accessibility**: In the past, video analysis was only available to teams competing at the professional level; however, it is now available to teams competing at all levels, from professionals to players in the Sunday League. By making this technology more accessible to the general public, amateur and lower-league teams, and even Sunday league players who have aspirations of winning a cup, are able to use the same technologies that professional sportsmen utilize. It is becoming more apparent that video analysis is not only a passing fad; rather, it is a revolutionary force that is influencing the future of coaching. This is because the effect of video analysis is spreading across all levels of sports.

It can be concluded that sports video analysis is not only useful but also an absolute need in the modern coaching environment. In addition, as technology continues to progress, its advantages are trickling down to grassroots levels, guaranteeing that no team, regardless of its magnitude, is left behind in the quest for greatness. Its broad acceptance in professional circles is a monument to the effect that it has had

Conclusion

In this book, we have examined the most important aspects of touch rugby, providing ideas that can offer the basis for success in the game. We've seen all the basic rules of touch rugby, comparing them and pointing out the differences with traditional rugby. Every player, coach, and fan should know the fundamental concepts and elements of the game well to participate or follow the game in a way that will make the most out of it.

We talked about the offensive and defensive end of the field and the game, mentioning tactics and schemes that could help the coaching staff, players, and teams as a whole prepare and work on plans of their own to maximize their potential. As we said, individual talent and improvement must be combined with teamwork and communication in order for the team to flourish and achieve the best possible outcome.

Knowing your own strengths and weaknesses is crucial, and the same is true for the strengths and weaknesses of the opponent. The game is not only played. It is also studied, prepared, thought, and planned. Coaches and players must be able to read each other and the opposition in order to achieve cohesion and effective collaboration and create problems or neutralize the opposition altogether.

We provided a great number of drills that can be used for individual practice and development, as well as drills useful for teamwork. We also covered tactics and strategies from the basic to the more advanced level.

A book can help explain rules, concepts, and ideas and provide examples and schemes with which a team can work. However, touch rugby, like every other sport, is ultimately a practical and athletic activity. What will decide a player's or coach's success will be their work and insistence on the field, not just the theoretical knowledge. That's not to say that theory is secondary in touch rugby and sport, but to put the attention on the practical implementation and work. Theory can only be important for a sportsman as far as it is accompanied by practice and commitment.

On the other hand, theory can be essential for fans who want to understand the game better, although they don't have the experience of playing or at least not playing on a higher level. The book can help fans who have developed a larger interest in touch rugby enjoy the game more, and in case they seek to enter the field, give them all the basic knowledge they need to begin their journey in the sport.

Touch rugby is a game that exemplifies inclusiveness and adaptation, and it stands out among the many different aspects that make up the landscape of rugby, embedding the essence of rugby while also leading the way for a community of players. Touch rugby is distinct for its inclusivity, as perhaps more than any other team sport, it is open to different ages, levels of physical condition, genders, and personal traits. It's a game that celebrates movement, speed, enjoyment, communication, timing, and many other elements that can bring people together to compete in a safe, fun, and fair way.

References

5 Benefits of sports video analysis. (n.d.). Nacsport. https://www.nacsport.com/blog/en-us/Tips/benefits-sports-video-analysis

Admin. (2016, July 7). *Benefits of Sport Performance Video analysis.* Tim Turk Hockey. https://www.timturkhockey.com/benefits-of-sport-performance-video-analysis/

Antonio. (2023, April 14). *Why is video analysis so important for the development of young athletes?* Once. https://once.de/blog/why-is-video-analysis-so-important-for-the-development-of-young-athletes/

Ashford, M., Abraham, A., & Poolton, J. (2021). What cognitive mechanism, when, where, and why? Exploring the decision making of university and professional rugby union players during competitive matches. *Frontiers in Psychology*, 12. https://doi.org/10.3389/fpsyg.2021.609127

Attack. (n.d.). Otago Touch Association. https://www.otagotouch.co.nz/Development-1/Coaching-Tips/Attacking-Tips

Beaven, R. P., Highton, J., Thorpe, M., Knott, E. V., & Twist, C. (2014). Movement and physiological demands of international and regional men's touch rugby matches. *The Journal of Strength and Conditioning Research*, 28(11), 3274–3279. https://doi.org/10.1519/jsc.0000000000000535

Breen, P. (2023, August 23). *Endurance training for rugby: Building stamina for peak performance.* Rugby Bricks. https://rugbybricks.com/en-gb/blogs/rugby-training/endurance-training-for-rugby-building-stamina-for-peak-performance

By Editor & Editor. (2022, May 22). *What is Touch Rugby? 2022 Easy to Understand Guide for the sport.* INTOUCH RUGBY. https://www.intouchrugby.com/magazine/what-is-touch-rugby-2022-easy-to-understand-guide-for-the-sport/

Campo, M., Champely, S., Lane, A. M., Rosnet, É., Ferrand, C., & Louvet, B. (2019). Emotions and performance in rugby. *Journal of Sport and Health Science*, 8(6), 595–600. https://doi.org/10.1016/j.jshs.2016.05.007

Clark, A. (2023, June 15). *Crunching the Codes: Tag Rugby vs. Touch Rugby vs. Full Contact Rugby.* Rugbystuff. https://www.rugbystuff.com/blogs/rugby-stuff-news/crunching-the-codes-tag-rugby-vs-touch-rugby-vs-full-contact-rugby

The 3 Benefits of Video Analysis. (n.d.). CoachNow Blog. https://coachnow.io/blog/tpost/pgc2lin221-the-3-benefits-of-video-analysis

Colomer, C., Pyne, D. B., Mooney, M., McKune, A. J., & Serpell, B. G. (2020). Performance Analysis in Rugby Union: a Critical Systematic Review. *Sports Medicine - Open*, 6(1). https://doi.org/10.1186/s40798-019-0232-x

Cottrell, D. (n.d.). *Rugby coaching tips to develop an offensive move.* Rugby Coach Weekly.

https://www.rugbycoachweekly.net/rugby-drills-and-skills/attack/rugby-coaching-tips-to-develop-an-offensive-move

Cottrell, D. (n.d., a). *Touch rugby basics.* Rugby Coach Weekly. https://www.rugbycoachweekly.net/rugby-drills-and-skills/touch-tag-sevens/touch-rugby-basics

Cottrell, D. (n.d., b). *Touch rugby to teach players defence.* Rugby Coach Weekly. https://www.rugbycoachweekly.net/rugby-drills-and-skills/defence/touch-rugby-to-teach-players-defence

Cottrell, D. (n.d., c). *Touch rugby top tips.* Rugby Coach Weekly. https://www.rugbycoachweekly.net/rugby-drills-and-skills/touch-tag-sevens/touch-rugby-top-tips

Cox, C. T. (2021, July 24). *8 Rugby Post-Game recovery Methods.* PowerHouse Rugby. https://www.powerhouserugby.com/8-rugby-post-game-recovery-methods/

Dale, P. (2020, February 7). *After rugby games, eat to recover.* Ruck Science. https://ruckscience.com/learn/after-rugby-game-eat-to-recover/

Defensive touch warm up - Rugby drills, rugby coaching. (n.d.). Sportplan. https://www.sportplan.net/drills/Rugby/Warm-Up/Defensive-Touch-rcd61.jsp

Department of Health & Human Services. (n.d.). *Touch football - preventing injury.* Better Health Channel. https://www.betterhealth.vic.gov.au/health/healthyliving/touch-football-preventing-injury

Dunnill, A. (n.d.). *Touch fitness training rugby drills*, videos. SportPlan. https://www.sportplan.net/s/Rugby/touch-fitness-training.jsp

Eaton, C., & George, K. (2006). Position specific rehabilitation for rugby union players. Part I: Empirical movement analysis data. *Physical Therapy in Sport*, 7(1), 22–29. https://doi.org/10.1016/j.ptsp.2005.08.006

Eaves, J. S., & Evers, L. (2007). The relationship between the 'play the ball' time, post-ruck action and the occurrence of perturbations in professional rugby league football. *International Journal of Performance Analysis in Sport*, 7(3), 18–25. https://doi.org/10.1080/24748668.2007.11868406

Farrar, J. (2019, August 9). *Common tag Rugby injuries*. *Physiotherapy & Sports Injury Clinics*. The Physio Company. https://www.thephysiocompany.com/blog/2019/8/9/common-tag-rugby-injuries

Focus On The Touch Rugby. (n.d.). Rugby Corner. https://rugby-corner.com/en/test/6_focus-on-the-touch-rugby.html

Gooding, N. (n.d.). *July Coaching Tip - Touch Rugby Attacking Strategy*. Exeter Touch Rugby. https://www.pitchero.com/clubs/exetertouchrugby/news/july-coaching-tip--touch-rugby-attacking-strategy--1461833.html

Great player post match questions for Ready 4 Rugby. (n.d.). Rugby Coach Weekly.

https://www.rugbycoachweekly.net/return-to-play/great-player-post-match-questions-for-ready-4-rugby

Hollander, S. D., Jones, B., Lambert, M., & Hendricks, S. (2018). The what and how of video analysis research in rugby union: a critical review. *Sports Medicine - Open*, 4(1). https://doi.org/10.1186/s40798-018-0142-3

Howard, T. (2020, May 3). *Touch Rugby Training Guide*. Ruck Science. https://ruckscience.com/programs/touch-rugby-training-guide/

Indigo Books & Music Inc. (n.d.). *Touch Rugby: Everything you need to play and coach*. Indigo. https://www.indigo.ca/en-ca/touch-rugby-everything-you-need-to-play-and-coach/8D36E169-9C08-480C-A906-77DAB7E2E25D.html

Inspired Agency. (2023, August 29). *Tag Rugby Rules & How to Play*. Try Tag Rugby. https://www.trytagrugby.com/learn/tag-rugby-rules-how-to-play/

James, N., Mellalieu, S. D., & Jones, N. (2005). The development of position-specific performance indicators in professional rugby union. *Journal of Sports Sciences*, 23(1), 63–72. https://doi.org/10.1080/02640410410001730106

Kell, L. (n.d.). *Recovery from rugby*. Centurion Rugby. https://www.centurion-rugby.com/blogs/rugby/recovery-from-rugby

Lloyd, G. (2023, June 6). *Video Analysis in Sports: Benefits & How to Use*. Trace. https://traceup.com/benefits-of-video-analysis-sports

Mathesius, P., & Strand, B. (1994). Touch rugby: an alternative activity in physical education. *Journal of Physical Education, Recreation & Dance*, 65(4), 55–59. https://doi.org/10.1080/07303084.1994.10606899

Mouchet, A., Harvey, S., & Light, R. (2013). A study on in-match rugby coaches' communications with players: a holistic approach. *Physical Education and Sport Pedagogy*, 19(3), 320–336. https://doi.org/10.1080/17408989.2012.761683

Neumann, D. C., McCurdie, I., & Wade, A. J. (1998). A survey of injuries sustained in the game of Touch. *Journal of Science and Medicine in Sport*, 1(4), 228–235. https://doi.org/10.1016/s1440-2440(09)60006-2

Nichol, R. (2014, November 10). *Reading the play in attack: aligning in the gap*. Conversational Rugby. https://conversationalrugby.wordpress.com/2014/11/09/reading-the-play-in-attack-aligning-in-the-gap/

No ball touch - defence - under 10 drills - rugby toolbox. (n.d.). Rugby Toolbox. https://www.rugbytoolbox.co.nz/training/technique/no-ball-touch

Passing and handling rugby drills. (n.d.). Rugby Coach Weekly. https://www.rugbycoachweekly.net/rugby-drills-and-skills/passing-handling

Patel, O. (n.d.). *Pasha 122: How video analysis benefits rugby*. The Conversation. https://theconversation.com/pasha-122-how-video-analysis-benefits-rugby-166913

Peterson, P. (2018, July 17). *The benefits of video analysis in Rugby*. Medium. https://medium.com/@peterpeterson_76117/the-benefits-of-video-analysis-in-rugby-a3277722617b

Players of all ages and abilities encouraged to take up Touch Rugby League. (n.d.). Rugby-League. https://www.rugby-league.com/article/61466/players-of-all-ages-and-abilities-encouraged-to-take-up-touch-rugby-league

Quarrie, K. L., Hopkins, W. G., Anthony, M. J., & Gill, N. (2013). Positional demands of international rugby union: Evaluation of player actions and movements. *Journal of Science and Medicine in Sport*, 16(4), 353–359. https://doi.org/10.1016/j.jsams.2012.08.005

Rae, K. (n.d.). *Four benefits of Video Analysis that aren't immediately obvious*. Couch Logic. https://www.coach-logic.com/blog/four-benefits-of-video-analysis-that-arent-immediately-obvious

Reardon, C., Tobin, D. P., & Delahunt, E. (2015). Application of individualized speed thresholds to interpret position specific running demands in Elite Professional Rugby Union: a GPS study. *PLOS ONE*, 10(7), e0133410. https://doi.org/10.1371/journal.pone.0133410

Ruck Science. (2023, November 29). *Post-Rugby - the rugby recovery formula*. Ruck Science. https://ruckscience.com/supplements/post-game/

Rugby basics. (n.d.). Marin Highlanders Rugby Club. https://www.marinhighlandersrugby.org/page/show/3386252-rugby-basics

Rugby handling Drills & coaching videos. (n.d.). RugbyIQ. http://www.rugbyiq.com/videos/handling/

Rules. (2022, August 6). TRL. https://www.trl.com.au/about/rules/

Spencer, B. (n.d.). *My weaknesses in tackling and passing and what I can learn from elite players.* Marked by Teachers. https://www.markedbyteachers.com/as-and-a-level/physical-education-sport-and-coaching/rugby-analysis-my-weaknesses-in-tackling-and-passing-and-what-i-can-learn-from-elite-players.html

Sullivan, P. J. (n.d.). *The relationship between communication and cohesion in inter-collegiate rugby players.* Scholarship at UWindsor. https://scholar.uwindsor.ca/etd/4204

The difference between touch rugby and regular rugby. (2020, December 16). Touch Rugby League. https://www.playtouchrugbyleague.co.uk/the-difference-between-touch-rugby-and-regular-rugby/

The rules. (2024, January 3). England Touch. https://www.englandtouch.org.uk/develop/coaching/the-rules/

Weisman, T. (n.d.). *Pump fakes and clearing.* Theodore Weisman. http://websites.umich.edu/~tjwei/frisbee/pumpfake.html#:~:text=You%20decide%20that%20the%20potential,called%20the%20%22pump%20fake.%22

Touch Defense. (n.d.). Sportplan.
	https://www.sportplan.net/sketches/Rugby/openSketch/4089073

Touch Rugby. (2007, November 23).
	https://web.uvic.ca/~thopper/WEB/452/Units_2007/Mark_Chris/Site/Lesson_4/Entries/2007/11/23__Final_Progression_TOUCH_RUGBY.html

Touch Rugby Rules - Utah Warriors Rugby. (2020, August 20). Utah Warriors Rugby.
	https://www.warriorsrugby.com/touch-rugby-rules

Touch Rugby Rules | Complete guide on how to play. (2018, November 9). GO Mammoth.
	https://www.gomammoth.co.uk/touch-rugby/rules

Touch Rugby rules: how to play, basic rules. (n.d.). Sportsmatik.
	https://sportsmatik.com/sports/touch-rugby/rules

What is Touch Rugby? (n.d.). RCBRS.
	https://rcbrs.de/en/teams/touch/

Training for sports - touch rugby. (n.d.). Revolutions Fit.
	https://revolutions.fit/blog/training-for-sports-touch-rugby

Performance analysis. (n.d.). WJEC.
	http://resource.download.wjec.co.uk.s3.amazonaws.com/vtc/2015-16/15-16_30/eng/03-post-match/Unit3-performance-analysis.html

Using video analysis in sports practices. (n.d.). TeamSnap.
	https://www.teamsnap.com/blog/general-sports/benefits-of-using-video-analysis-in-sports-practices

Why is video analysis important in sport? (n.d.). Veo Sports Camera. https://www.veo.co/article/the-importance-of-video-analysis-in-sport

Non Contact. (2023, August 1). World Rugby. https://www.world.rugby/the-game/game-participation/get-into-rugby/non-contact/?

Printed in Great Britain
by Amazon